Fifty & Friendless

Table for One Please!

Friendships, Farewells
and Finding YOU

JEN MORGAN

with Diana Acosta

DOVE
PUBLISHING HOUSE

Fifty & Friendless: Table For One Please
Copyright © 2025 Jen Morgan
All rights reserved.

No part of this book may be reproduced or used in any manner without written permission of the copyright owner or publisher except for the use of quotations in a book review.

Disclaimer: The representation of views, opinions, and beliefs contained in this book do not reflect the views, opinions, or beliefs of anyone other than the author.

For information, inquiries, or permissions, please contact:
Dove Publishing House
www.dovepublishinghouse.com

Book cover and design by Sadie Butterworth-Jones

ISBN (Paperback): 978-1-960807-26-7
ISBN (Hardback): 978-1-960807-27-4

Scripture quotations marked (ESV) are from the ESV® Bible (The Holy Bible, English Standard Version®), © 2001 by Crossway, a publishing ministry of Good News Publishers. ESV Text Edition: 2025. Used by permission. All rights reserved.

Scripture quotations marked (MEV) are taken from THE HOLY BIBLE, MODERN ENGLISH VERSION, copyright © 2014 by Military Bible Association. Published and distributed by Charisma House.

Scripture quotations marked (NIV) are taken from the Holy Bible, New International Version®, NIV®. Copyright © 1973, 1978, 1984, 2011 by Biblica, Inc.™ Used by permission of Zondervan. All rights reserved worldwide.

Scripture quotations marked (NKJV) are taken from the New King James Version®. Copyright © 1982 by Thomas Nelson. Used by permission. All rights reserved.

Scripture quotations marked (NLT) are taken from the *Holy Bible*, New Living Translation, copyright © 1996, 2004, 2015 by Tyndale House Foundation. Used by permission of Tyndale House Publishers, Carol Stream, Illinois 60188. All rights reserved.

To my dear friend Pam –
From little girls in Cincinnati to wives, mothers, and everything in between, you were a constant, a light, and a staple in my life. Though we lost you too soon, your spirit still anchors us, guiding and watching over the rest of us. The memories of you will never fade.

Pam and Jen Morgan

To my Panther Posse –
No matter the miles or the years, you all will remain my steady reminder that even in grief, I have never truly been friendless. The revival of our bond has carried me through, and Pam's love will always live on in us.

Jen and her hometown "posse"

*To my sisters by blood and my sisters by choice –
I thank you for loving me, accepting me, and supporting me for exactly who I am, even when I don't make it very easy. I thank God for each one of you every day, and I pray I will be the friend to you that you so lovingly have been to me.*

Jen and her sisters

In Mark 2, Jesus healed a paralyzed man because of his FRIEND'S faith. This is why your circle matters.

*Love, Laughter, and Who Dey,
Jen*

Contents

Introduction xi

Foreword 15

Chapter 1: The Mirror 17
    It All Starts with Me 21
    How Can I Be the Friend I Crave? 24
    Self-Talk 26
    Quality Versus Quantity 28
    Satisfy Your Cravings 30
    The Beautiful Gift of Friendship — Are You Ready? 34

Chapter 2: The Friendship Food Pyramid: Who's Filling Your Plate? 39

    Meal Prep Madness 40

    The Friendship App 43

    The Acquaintance 45

    The Casual/Social 47

    The Bestie 49

    Intimate/Family #Ditchdiver 54

    Journal Reflection: The Heart of Friendship 59

    Let's Take It a Little Further 60

    Conclusion 60

Chapter 3: Grief In Life and Death 65

    Grief Is Personal 69

    Exchange Grief for Gratitude 71

    Being Selective with Your Tears 73

    Diana's Story 75

Chapter 4: Oils of Renewal 81

    The Eyes Are the Window of the Soul 83

    The Mirror Screamed 84

    I Did Not Sign Up for This 85

    The Fairy Tale 90

    Even Queens Grieve 91

Aromatherapy with Purpose 93
How Does This Apply to Us? 93
Six Months of Perfume and Preparation — The Spa Life 96

Chapter 5: Fashion, Forgiveness, and Letting Go 101
Let's Talk the "F-Word" 104
Letting Go Without Snapping the Strap 106

Chapter 6: Table for One Please! 123
Love Affair 130
Flying Not-So-Solo 132
1. Set Clear Goals 134
2. Develop a Routine 135
3. Self-Reflection 135
4. Prioritize Health 136
5. Combatting Mental Health Stigma 136
Space For You and the Ultimate Friend 138

About the Author 143

Introduction

Beautiful Friend,

Welcome to Fifty & Friendless!

At first glance, the title of this book may be a bit confusing, causing you to wonder if you will suddenly become friendless as you hit your fabulous 50's. The answer to that is NO! However, when you dive into the journey of friendship I am sharing with you, I hope you'll emerge with a new perspective on cherishing those deep bonds you have formed through the years — most importantly, the one you have with yourself.

My husband, Kevin, loves to tease me. He always has. Let's just say it's part of his charm. After going through difficult friendship experiences within the past few years, he began playfully calling me "no-friend Jen" and "fifty & friendless." Two nicknames that might seem cruel to some, but because I know how to laugh at my own circumstances, I actually found them quite humorous. It was his quirky but loving way of encouraging me to laugh when the tears were starting to consume me.

After some time and a lot of self-reflection, I realized that it was the perfect title of my new book on the value of friendships as we age.

As you join me on this journey of discovering the value of quality over quantity in female relationships, I pray that you will become more aware of your own value. Though your stories are your own and only you know the depths of what you might be yearning for, I pray that what I am sharing with you inspires you to delve a bit deeper.

Our hearts are delicate, ladies, and we must protect them without hardening them due to loss, rejection, or grief. Continuing to grow through these challenges will support your quest for a more intimate relationship with the women in your life, with yourself, and with Jesus — the ultimate in an invaluable spiritual friendship.

You have picked up this book because at some point you have found yourself battling with a lack of companionship in the way of friends. You may have been hurt, or you may have found yourself on the other side of the suffering, and you are seeking grace. I invite

INTRODUCTION

you to be vulnerable with yourself: open your heart to this new season in life and what God has in store for you.

Whether you are surrounded by five, twelve, or twenty friends, it is most important to be the person that *you* crave and to cherish that person every single day.

Cheers to us finding friendship with ourselves.

Love, Jen

Foreword

When I first heard the title *Fifty and Friendless*, I was taken aback. As women and social beings, the term friendless is something we usually avoid at all costs. Loneliness is something we tend to keep hidden in the corners of our hearts. It's the quiet ache many live with but few dare to speak about. That's what makes this book and encouraging memoir so extraordinary. Jen goes there! She shares the insight and wisdom she has learned and the truths that will carry you through to a real and lasting love and friendship with YOU.

This is not just a story about being fifty or being friendless. It is a story about the human need for connection and about rediscovering one's worth when the mirror of friendship is no longer there to reflect it back. The truth is we have to love ourselves or we cannot love anyone else. So many of us forget that!

In these pages, you will meet someone who chose to be courageous instead of comfortable. When Jen speaks about the masks we wear and her tear-filled seasons, she is choosing honesty over appearances, and vulnerability over silence. You will find moments that might make you nod in recognition, feel tears slipping down your cheeks or you might laugh out loud. I know I did! But most importantly, you will discover that you are not alone, even in loneliness, because you can cultivate a friendship with yourself, and we have a best friend, Jesus, who will never leave us or forsake us.

This book is not a lament. It is an invitation. An invitation to look at your own story with compassion and to accept that life rarely follows the plan or timelines we might imagine, but in every season God is good and His love for us will never fail.

Jennifer Weiss

Author of *Holy Spirit Adventures God at Work in the Marketplace* and host of the Grace Grit Glory Show

Chapter 1

The Mirror

"Mirror, mirror, on the wall, who's the fairest of them all?"

"Try this: Stand in front of a mirror each morning for one minute, look yourself directly in the eye, and listen to what the man or woman in the mirror says to you. It will make you uncomfortable. But it works."
~ Matthew Kelly

When reflecting on Matthew Kelly's wise words, I instantly feel the love/hate relationship I have with my own mirror. I love it because it reveals a woman with radiant confidence and contagious joy. On the surface, I see a flawless foundation, a fashionable outfit, and maybe even the reward of a few pounds lost. It's easy to smile at the polished version of myself.

But I also hate the mirror, because beyond the glam, it speaks to me in a voice I've come to know too well — harsh, unforgiving, and unkind. It points out the parts of me I wish I could ignore: the flaws I try to cover, the insecurities I try to silence, the wounds I thought had healed. It doesn't just reflect my image — it reminds me of everything I'm still trying to fix. I see the woman who doubts herself, who makes mistakes, who sometimes wants to run back to hiding behind the mask. I've stood in front of that mirror and felt the sting of my own self-judgment. No matter how perfect the look, I can't hide from the parts of me that feel unworthy, insecure, or not enough. The glam no longer matters when all I can see staring back at me is the inner ugly self. I am a work in progress — and it's very possible I always will be. But one thing I know for certain: I rely fully on the One who began a good work in me, and He's not finished yet.

> Being confident of this very thing, that He who has begun a good work in you will complete it until the day of Jesus Christ.
> **(Philippians 1:6 NKJV)**

CHAPTER 1: THE MIRROR

In one of my favorite childhood fairy tales, "Snow White and the Seven Dwarfs," the infamous mirror belonged to the Wicked Queen, who asked it the same question every day: "Mirror, mirror, on the wall, who's the fairest of them all?" And every day, the mirror responded in the same way: "My Queen, you are the fairest in the land."

Why she needed to ask this question repeatedly is worth speculating. The Wicked Queen asked the mirror every day, "Who is the fairest of them all?" not because she didn't already know the answer but because she was addicted to being affirmed, obsessed with remaining the most beautiful, and deeply insecure about losing her worth. Her identity was rooted in comparison. The mirror didn't just reflect her image; it also fed her ego and confirmed her value only when it aligned with her need to be the best. In many ways, that mirror became her idol — her daily source of identity. And when it no longer gave her the answer she wanted, it exposed just how fragile and unstable her sense of self really was.

So why did she ask?

Because she didn't believe she was enough unless someone (or something) confirmed it.

It's a cautionary tale, especially for us today. When we allow mirrors — whether literal, digital, or emotional — to define our worth, we'll always be enslaved to their response. And like the

Queen, we might find ourselves chasing "fairest" instead of healing what's fractured.

It wasn't until Snow White appeared that we saw a stark contrast: a young woman whose inner beauty radiated peace and joy instead of being stuck on appearances. Sadly, the Queen's downfall came from never realizing that true beauty flows from within and requires a far more honest, magnified lens to be seen clearly. That kind of lens can be terrifying. It forces us to face the parts of ourselves we'd rather keep hidden.

For those who've grown comfortable behind a mask, the idea of being fully seen — flaws and all — can feel overwhelming. And might I add, this often deepens with aging. We are no longer looking at the image we grew so familiar with over the years. We may not love what we see on our legs, our arms, or our backside. But the real question is this: Can we still love the woman in the mirror? Can we extend to her the same grace we so easily offer others? Can we move beyond what we no longer admire externally and choose instead to honor the beauty that's unfolding within?

"Mirror, mirror, on the wall" has been imposed on us by society, creating a huge issue of never measuring up. We need to break free from that! Allow the wisdom that comes with age to steer you away from the trap and embrace freedom!

CHAPTER 1: THE MIRROR

Freedom doesn't come from hiding; it comes from surrendering the mask and allowing God to define what's truly beautiful.

The mirror is simply a reflection, and though it can give a glimpse of beauty at a fleeting glance, the metaphor of the mirror depicts the root not only of our joys and positive attributes but also of our disappointments and heartache. Given that truth, shall we then consider that these moments at the mirror could be used as an opportunity to dig deeper into our experiences, our flaws, and our personal growth, specifically in the matter of our relationships with others? I believe that in examining ourselves outwardly, self-awareness gets lost in the bright light of our reflection. In times of conflict, rather than falling prey to the "mirror, mirror on the wall" temptation of seeking external validation, we would do well to honestly examine our own reflections and make a more genuine assessment of what lies beneath.

IT ALL STARTS WITH ME

My 50th birthday was more than a milestone celebration; it was an eye-opening and life-changing realization. The party décor was filled with rose gold, glitz, and champagne, surrounded by my kids, my husband, and some of my dearest friends. Finally, my Texas friends were meeting my "Panther Posse" from elementary school in Cincinnati. I felt like I was on top of the world and overwhelmed by joy, celebrating life with the people I truly loved and adored. If they weren't family by blood, they were family by choice. That is how I value friendship. The music was playing, cocktails were flowing, and laughter was echoing throughout the house and the patio, where we danced and took tons of photos — because if you know me, well, you know I love the photos! Making memories is my thing! The night was blissful and everything I could hope for a milestone birthday to be.

Suddenly, just months after such a blissful milestone, I was blindsided. What should've remained a season of joy and reflection quickly turned into one of unexpected pain. I found myself staring into the dreaded internal mirror — one I had managed to avoid for years. Close friendships began to fade, slipping away quietly, almost without explanation. One moment we were laughing, celebrating, doing life together — and the next, I was alone, left with nothing but unanswered questions and the reflection of a woman trying to make sense of it all.

I wanted to point the finger, to blame circumstances or the people who walked away. But eventually, the question turned inward: "Why did they abandon me?"

The joy of my 50th birthday, the celebration of half a century lived, was quickly overshadowed by grief and a deep sense of rejection. What should have been a time of grounding and grace instead left a painful void. I found myself asking the question I thought I had grown past: "What's wrong with me?"

CHAPTER 1: THE MIRROR

In my book *Bring It On* (chapter 2), I reveal how I became the mask master. I shared how I dominated the ability to wear a mask to camouflage the pain from the past buried in my heart. I wear masks of perfection, when in reality I am deeply flawed. I wear a mask of confidence, when I am swimming in insecurity. I wear a mask of being a true Christian woman, when at times, I feel I am living a life of hypocrisy. I mastered these masks, all the while desiring to rip them off and be free from the facade. I was bound by them. The masks became my identity.

In an age of social media saturation, unbeknownst to me, my masks were being virtually replaced with filters, which are conveniently at our fingertips, tempting us to project anything we desire. How do we escape the slippery slope of building a business and a brand while wanting to live out someone else's highlight reel? It's not an easy juggling act, but the simple answer is learning to accept and love the woman in the mirror in her truest form. The most common knee-jerk reaction when things don't go our way is to point the finger at someone else. I asked, "How can I shift the blame so that I don't have to address how I contributed to the strife?" When we do that, we fail to improve ourselves, therefore requiring less from others, and the cycle continues.

The reflection in the metaphorical mirror is not the same as it was twenty, ten, or even five years ago. There's a new image staring back at me. Forget the additional wrinkles and extra "layers" in places where they used to be non-existent. What is more meaningful is that where there was once a lack of confidence and insecurity, there is now a woman of authenticity, ready and willing to accept the best and worst in what she embodies. She is learning to show grace, love, and mercy to the outward appearance of the woman in the mirror. It is never easy, but a much harsher reality is dissecting her from the inside out. That is precisely what I was forced to do since my epic birthday celebration entering my 50's, and girl, if you're at a crossroads with meaningful friendships in your life, I am going to challenge you to do the same.

HOW CAN I BE THE FRIEND I CRAVE?

"I've learned that people will forget what you said, people will forget what you did, but people will never forget how you made them feel."
~ Maya Angelou

Through my older and, for the sake of argument, wiser years, I've truly learned to take a deep dive into myself and live more authentically as a woman, a Christian, a wife, sister, mother, and friend. This journey of self-love and self-acceptance has made me face the truth about the deception I had allowed to distort my self-image. It hasn't been easy. There were moments when the mirror reflected more pain than progress — reminders of how long I had measured my worth by comparison, perfectionism, and silent self-criticism.

CHAPTER 1: THE MIRROR

But self-examination became non-negotiable. Digging into the truths about who I am, both the beautiful and broken, was no longer optional. It was mandatory for growth. Little by little, I began to see transformation. I started to become someone **I could be proud of — not because I was perfect, but because I was real.** Fairly "maskless" and finally loving the girl being unveiled. Not flawless, but free. Not finished, but finally honest.

If you find yourself on this journey of uncovering the value of quality friendships as you mature, the first part of the challenge begins with befriending yourself. What does that even mean? To befriend yourself means learning to treat yourself with the same kindness, patience, and grace you so freely offer others. It's choosing to stand by your own side, not only in moments of strength but especially in moments of struggle, reminding your soul that you are worthy of love and gentleness, even from yourself. Work on becoming your own best friend! This may be a weird concept for some, but let's walk through it together. I truly believe that if we don't learn to love and respect ourselves, if we neglect our own needs and well-being, it becomes nearly impossible to offer that same love and care to others in a healthy way.

So let me ask: How do you treat yourself in the morning? I'm not talking about your coffee routine or how many times you hit snooze. I mean those first moments when your eyes open — what do you say to yourself? How do you greet your day?

Do you immediately fall into a pattern of self-criticism before your feet even hit the floor? Does the mirror feel more like a reminder of flaws than a reflection of God's grace? Or do you wake with a grateful heart, acknowledging the gift of a new day and offering praise to the One who gave it — regardless of what the next twenty-four hours may bring?

SELF-TALK

For months, I repeatedly woke up telling myself I wasn't good enough and that I was so flawed that I managed to run people off whom I believed to be some of my best and lifelong friends. That takes some real talent! Through all of the sleepless nights and countless tears I cried, overthinking and wondering,

Why would they abandon me?
What is wrong with me?
I thought we were lifers, family — what went wrong?

I was consumed with self-doubt and negativity; I spiraled downward, believing the lies of the enemy. That malicious devil really knows how to toy with our innermost thoughts and emotions, and boy, did he do a number on me! Words and thoughts are powerful seeds. When we engage in negative self-talk, we are sowing seeds into our minds and hearts. Seeds eventually bear fruit. If you sow a negative seed, you will reap rotten fruit.

CHAPTER 1: THE MIRROR

My friend, God does not create rotten fruit, nor did He create you to be anything less than the workings of His beautiful craftsmanship. Relish that for a moment. Indulge yourself in the idea that you are His daughter, and you are a unique and special individual with so much to offer. Once those truths penetrate your thoughts, they will spill over not only into your relationship with others, but more importantly, with the relationship you have with yourself. The question I pose to you now is, "What kind of friend do you crave, and how can you be her?"

If you are to be the friend you crave, then the first step is tapping into what God says about self-respect and the value of friendship.

> Since God chose you to be the holy people he loves, you must clothe yourselves with tenderhearted mercy, kindness, humility, gentleness, and patience. Make allowance for each other's faults, and forgive anyone who offends you. Remember, the Lord forgave you, so you must forgive others. Above all, clothe yourselves with love, which binds us all together in perfect harmony.
> **(Colossians 3:12–14 NLT)**

This passage speaks volumes, and I highly encourage you to stop what you're doing, grab a sticky note or index card, write it down, and hang it wherever you will see it every single day, preferably on your mirror (wink, wink). It is a colossal reminder for me to follow

God's instruction on loving, forgiving, and accepting myself and then having that same love, forgiveness, and acceptance for the people in my life. This realization did not come easy; it has come with adversity, experience, and dare I say, maturity. My purpose in writing this book is to closely examine the ways in which we grow and change in our relationships and how our values continuously evolve over time. Therefore, it is vital that we remain in touch with our soul, our strengths, and our weaknesses to bring out our best version of what it means to be a friend.

QUALITY VERSUS QUANTITY

I cannot proceed without telling you how incredibly blessed I am for the friendships I have acquired throughout my 54 years. As a child, a teen, and even in the more recent past, I was always surrounded by a big, wide, eclectic circle of people. Being the youngest of nine, would you expect any different? I embraced the joy, laughter, and fun of bringing people together to celebrate life and the little things. "The more the merrier" was my motto! The ability to gather people was what I believed to be one of God's gifts to me, a strength that I fully accepted and thrived upon. (I touch on this topic in chapter 6 of *Bring It On*.) As the years have gone by, the circles have gotten smaller, more intimate, but the values of the friendships remain intact. The women in my life whom I've known since I was a child and teen have seen it all with me. They know my strengths, they know my weaknesses, they

CHAPTER 1: THE MIRROR

know my ridiculous insecurities, and they know that I'll be the one in heels and with my hair done at a football game! They love me, accept me, and forgive me, because they know it is what I do for them. The same applies to my four incredible sisters. We are all cut from the same parental cloth, yet we are individuals, with distinctive qualities that set us apart. They know I crave attention and always need to be heard or get the laugh. They know I'm loud and never back down if I think I'm right. They know I mess up, but they know I'm doing my best. They love me, they accept me, and they forgive me.

Then there are those beautiful and rare individuals I have come to know throughout my years in Texas. The women of all ages, backgrounds, occupations, religions, and marital status, women whom I've met by the grace of God. He has hand-picked and delivered them into my life at just the right time, and I cherish them with all my heart. Whether it be a birthday lunch, an impromptu glass (or bottle) of wine, a girl's night out, pool day, Bible study, or those unforgettable week-after-week, year-after-year wine chats on the sofa, these ladies get me, and they love me, accept me, and forgive me, because they know it is exactly what I do for them.

Let me be crystal clear: I do not believe all friendships are meant to last forever. I am not so gullible as to believe that people will remain as close to me today as they were in years past. Seasons change, people move, kids grow, values develop, and we mature and discover that it may be time to move on. That is okay! You may even get the old "It's not you, it's me" spiel. It is genuinely okay for seasons to change in friendship even as you keep them in your heart.

Then there are those who just stick, gel, or vibe! Those are the ones who will stand the test of time when you fall short; through the hiccups and inevitable changes, the love remains. They are the ones who will challenge you, confront you, and force you to face truths about yourself that you want to hide from. Begrudgingly, these are the ones we allow to hold up the mirror when we want to look away. These are the friendships of blood, sweat, and tears — better known as the "ditch divers." They are invaluable.

> *"The friends who have seen every version you have ever been, from that rock bottom broken to that sky-high heaven and everything in between, and stayed through it all, hold them now, hold them forever."*
> **~ Stephanie Bennett-Henry**

SATISFY YOUR CRAVINGS

In preparation for this book, I realized I can only speak from my own experiences, and though I have a plethora in this regard, I knew it would be important to get the perspective of other women. I mean, what better group of people to poll than the audience I'm writing for? One question I posed in doing research was, "What

CHAPTER 1: THE MIRROR

qualities did you value in a friend in your teens or younger years, and what qualities do you value now?" There was a common thread for both ages. In our younger years, most of us searched for friends with common interests, who were fun, trustworthy or good at keeping secrets, and inclusive. Nobody wanted to be left out. FOMO (fear of missing out) has always been a thing, ladies! As maturity sets in, what we treasure tends to evolve; however, loyalty remains the common theme.

The other things I found that most women search for in friendship are honesty, respect, authenticity, acceptance, and compassion or empathy. I am confident the fun factor goes without saying. These qualities are no small component in a healthy, compatible friendship. They give us a barometer in vetting whom we want to spend time with and whom we might want to pour more of ourselves into. Our time is valuable, and spending it with people who feed our souls and bring us joy should be a prerequisite. They're also not easy to find. Just like God is not a vending machine with our prayers, we're unable to press a few buttons of friendship qualifications and have that magical person suddenly pop into our lives. What we can do is invest the time in ourselves, do a deep self-exploration of what we crave, and become her!

Self-respect and self-awareness are two huge steps in this process. It's the ability not only to know and believe that you're worthy of having those quality people in your life but also to recognize you may have to take a hard look at yourself to make the necessary changes to attract and keep those women. I am in no way suggesting you become a chameleon to maintain relationships that are no longer bearing fruit. If you're familiar with my work, you know I am all about striving to be your best authentic self in all circumstances. I am, however, suggesting that you work on becoming who you crave through prayer, honest and raw self-talk, and maintaining self-respect throughout the journey.

When you practice self-respect, you will not settle for anything less than respect from others. Mutual respect is the foundation of any long-lasting friendship. It is the glue that keeps you together. Others will notice a shift in your behavior when you carry yourself with self-respect. They will notice something different exuding from your presence. Confidence is attractive in any setting! I can always tell when someone has a healthy self-esteem by the way they carry themselves and how they respond to others. I want to exude that confidence when people are around me, so I make sure to speak the right things into my heart and mind. But for a while, as friendships drifted, the confidence I worked so hard to maintain started to melt away, leading me to question what kind of friend I am and how I could be better. Through my journaling, my quiet talks with Jesus, and with the help of the women I deeply cherish, I've learned to slay negative thoughts when they creep into my mind, and I exchange them for truth. Because of my past insecurities, it has not been an easy road for me, but the more I befriend the woman in the mirror, the more I love her, accept her, and forgive her.

CHAPTER 1: THE MIRROR

What am I looking for in a friend? Loyalty, compassion, thoughtfulness, forgiveness, and grace. Most importantly, I crave the woman who will hold up the mirror in front of me and tell me what I *need* to hear, not what I *want* to hear, with gentleness and from a place of genuine care. If I can be her, then I have everything I need. In full transparency, my love language is words of affirmation, so as much as I love getting compliments, it brings me much greater joy to give them out! The art of loving who I am is a conscious act, and it is ongoing. It's been hard work, but I made the decision to look myself straight in the eye when I slip into negativity and, with the grace of God, make the necessary corrections. Believe me when I tell you, Jen on her own is just Jen. Jen with the help of almighty God is the one continually growing into a better version of herself. I haven't fully overcome, but I sure am giving it my best, and so can you.

Take a moment to articulate how you can be a better friend to yourself. What are you doing to grow as a person? What can you do differently to show yourself more love?

If you are having a hard time answering these questions, then let's take a few minutes to pray into this area of your life. It is impossible to attract the friend you crave without being that friend to yourself first.

Pray With Me
Father, I pray for the woman reading this page right now. She is struggling with self-love, self-care, self-worth, and self-respect. She may be focusing on her failures rather than her virtues. I pray You open her eyes to see the reflection of her beauty when she looks in the mirror — her inner beauty and her outer beauty. Heal every area of her life that has been wounded by others and wounded by her own decisions, so she may walk with confidence and a healthy self-esteem. Prepare her for the friends You will bring into her life, and prepare her to be the friend someone is craving. Amen.

From this moment on, you will not be the same. You are now on the path of authentic friendships. By being your own best friend, you are becoming the friend you crave, and you will attract like-minded friends. Friends who are also intentional about having healthy, long-lasting friendships.

THE BEAUTIFUL GIFT OF FRIENDSHIP — ARE YOU READY?

Friends are a gift from God! To preserve the beauty of friendship, we must be ready and willing to invest time and dedication in ourselves and in one another. Long-lasting, genuine friendship

CHAPTER 1: THE MIRROR

requires nurturing, honesty, and communication. Two-way communication is a must! A one-way street of communication is simply not sustainable, nor is it a healthy path by which a friendship can flourish. You need friends who will invest in you as much as you invest in them. Friends who will speak the truth in love from a genuine heart and have your best interest at heart, even if it isn't exactly what you want to hear. Only genuine friends have the courage to raise the mirror in honesty and love. It is so much easier to sweep things under the rug or look the other way. A genuine friend will never do that, because she is looking out for your best interest.

We were all created for companionship from the beginning of time. When Adam was alone in the garden, God made Eve. When Noah built the ark, the animals came in twos. There is purpose in companionship — not only the companionship of a spouse but also the companionship of a friend.

> Two are better than one, because there is a good reward for their labor together. For if they fall, then one will help up his companion. But woe to him who is alone when he falls and has no one to help him up.
> **(Ecclesiastes 4:9–12 MEV)**

Are you ready? Are you ready to welcome this person into your life, and are you ready to be her?

Reflections

When looking in the mirror, what friend qualities do you see looking back at you?

_____
_____
_____
_____
_____
_____
_____
_____
_____
_____
_____
_____
_____
_____
_____
_____
_____
_____

Chapter 2

The Friendship Food Pyramid: Who's Filling Your Plate?

If friendship were a food group, most of us might find ourselves starving in the wrong places. Some of the deepest friendships are built not just on trust and loyalty but also on coffee dates, lunches, and happy hours! Come on now! There's just something sacred about bonding over our favorite sushi rolls, having heart-to-hearts while splitting a pint of your favorite ice cream you swore you weren't going to eat, or toasting a win with a crisp glass of bubbles. **Food and friendship go hand in hand like mashed potatoes and gravy — comforting, dependable, and always better together.** In fact, I'm convinced food is the universal love language! We may say, "I'm here for you," but what we really mean is, "I've got the charcuterie, you bring the wine!"

So as we dive into what I like to call the "friendship pyramid," let's start at the base — where laughter, leftovers, and late-night cravings lay the foundation for something real.

MEAL PREP MADNESS

Are you a meal prep queen? Are you among the goddesses that map out the right proteins with the right carbs and know the difference between "good fats" and "fat fats?" Do you carefully review simple carbs versus complex carbs, while considering that one blogger says you should eat fruits but another blogger says you should not eat fruit at all? Your fitness coach swears by oatmeal in the morning, while your favorite influencer fiercely tells you to stay away from the oatmeal, and you should race home to eat within thirty minutes, otherwise your workout was a waste of time! After riding the meal prep roller coaster, you find yourself staring at the fridge, wondering what you can eat that is easy, simple, and will make your heart (and belly) happy, without throwing your waistline out the window! Sheesh — how do we keep it all straight?

CHAPTER 2: THE FRIENDSHIP FOOD PYRAMID

As funny as that may sound, it is a glimpse of what friendship and friendlessness can look like as we age! You want friends, but not too many friends. You crave quality time, but no one has any, because life is basically a sprint at this point. Then, when you finally do make plans, you suddenly realize you'd much rather be at home, hair in a bun, wearing your favorite stretchy pants, curled up with Netflix and zero expectations. Then, halfway through a show you're not even paying attention to, you start feeling a little lonely because you haven't seen those few precious friends in weeks. It's wild! You crave connection, but you desperately need your couch. Managing healthy friendships later in life, just like managing our metabolism, can be very complex and can start to feel like a juggling act.

Coming from someone who was used to being surrounded by a diverse group of friends, I reluctantly have discovered that less is more. I fought that concept tooth and nail for years. However, I have discovered that though I cherish the memories of "the good old days," I now embrace simple, straight-to-the-point loyalty and authenticity. Honest and loyal friendships are first found in being that person and later by carefully assessing or "friend prepping." How awesome would it be to throw all the qualities we want in our blender and create the perfect friend? Unfortunately, it doesn't happen that way. We must take the time to measure which "ingredients" we crave, and remember that adding more does not make for a miracle recipe. Some of my most delicious recipes only require three key ingredients. Most friends are not going to possess every single quality we desire or need, but that is what makes the discovery so much more inviting. Taking the time to consider what we really want and need is so vital to our friendship path.

FRIENDSHIP PYRAMID

Back in the day, I could eat whatever I wanted, and my waistline never blinked. Late-night chips and dip? Cheese fries at midnight? No problem — my jeans still fit in the morning. But oh, how times have changed. Thanks to menopause (and her rude cousin, hormones) every bite now counts. These days, I rely on walks, Pilates, and my Oura Ring just to keep my body in check. As for that extra glass of vino — well, we won't get into that.

Now, if we only had an app to help us discover the formula for our friendship's health and wellness status, we'd be in business. Something to calculate the perfect balance of time, energy, vulnerability, and boundaries. We need that pesky notification

CHAPTER 2: THE FRIENDSHIP FOOD PYRAMID

similar to our Oura Ring, reminding us, "Time to check in with your people." Navigating healthy friendships can feel just as complicated as tracking macros — maybe even more so.

THE FRIENDSHIP APP

I believe that "app" lies within our hearts and is powered by our years of experience. Let that sink in for a moment. Trial and error, shall we say? I have developed a sense in my soul of what I want, what I need, and what I bring to the equation to cultivate healthy friendships and truly embrace how that will enhance my life.

I start by understanding the importance of categorizing. Categorizing helps in minimizing premature emotional investment in a relationship. I cannot stress enough the importance of knowing someone before opening the doors to your heart and inner circle. The apostle Paul expressed it very wisely:

> When I was a child, I spoke as a child, I understood as a child, and I thought as a child. But when I became a man, I put away childish things.
> **(1 Corinthians 13:11 MEV)**

We can no longer afford to think or behave like we did on the playground. Back then, we welcomed everyone into our sandbox or onto the swing set without a second thought. Those were innocent days when we didn't see color, race, or status. We just played. Sure, there was the occasional neighborhood squabble, but full-on mean girl energy? That was rare.

Unfortunately, in these times of social media highlight reels and everyone striving to outdo one another, that mindset no longer fits. As we grow, we've got to develop healthier disciplines if we want friendships that last. Just like we're learning our macros and reading food labels, we've got to start *friend prepping* with the same level of intentionality. That means learning the art of categorizing. We've already done our self-checks in the mirror — now it's time to ask deeper questions about the people we allow into our lives:

- What's her main ingredient?
- What are her core values?
- Is she consistent?
- Does she keep her word?
- And here's a big one we rarely think about: How does she treat the servers, bartenders, and sales reps?

The most important questions are the ones tied to what *you* value most. It's your responsibility to compartmentalize and categorize before committing to any relationship.

You might be thinking, "Jen, is it worth all this effort? Shouldn't friendship just come naturally?"

CHAPTER 2: THE FRIENDSHIP FOOD PYRAMID

My quick answer? Yes, it *should*. Friendship should not require such heavy lifting. However, your heart is fragile. And if you lend it out too freely, the damage control afterward takes far more energy than the upfront work of being intentional. Trust me on that one.

So let's dive in a little deeper, shall we? In most cases, friendships will fall into four main categories:

1. Acquaintance
2. Casual/Social
3. Bestie
4. Intimate/Family #Ditchdiver

THE ACQUAINTANCE

I'm just going to put it out there — this is my least favorite place on the friendship pyramid, and I am not very good at it. Either because I believe it to be a waste of time and effort, or because I have learned to conserve my energy for more meaningful experiences. I'm learning as I go. An acquaintance is someone we know casually, with limited interaction. They may have been introduced through a mutual friend or neighbor, but they are not someone we find ourselves emotionally invested in. Conversations are often surface-level, and interactions may be limited to specific contexts like work, school, or social events. The relationship is often superficial and generally consists of small talk. We may not feel comfortable discussing personal matters or seeking emotional support from them, and we shouldn't — we just met! I'm sure we've all come across someone who overshares at that first introduction, and it can be uncomfortable. Let's not be that girl!

I know, I know; acquaintances do have their place in our friendship pyramid! They bring new experiences, diversity, and often, a whole lot of fun. We get the chance to ask questions, explore different industries and cultures, and ask questions like "Where are you from, and what team do you root for?" Rarely, but sometimes, those connections grow into something deeper. But it's important to keep them in the right category until you see more of a common thread.

Another perk of having acquaintances is networking potential. Maintaining a healthy network is key to your personal and professional growth. An acquaintance does not need to have the objective of moving into a bestie relationship, but putting yourself out there can lead to another intention. There are people who come into your life for one purpose and one purpose only. It is wise to identify what that is and nurture it accordingly, without a hidden agenda. Knowing the difference helps you set appropriate boundaries and manage expectations. By *boundaries*, I mean you should not immediately become her number one stalker on Instagram and new best friend on Facebook. Social media etiquette is a fine line to tread, so tread lightly. Avoid being a "friend collector."

CHAPTER 2: THE FRIENDSHIP FOOD PYRAMID

THE CASUAL/SOCIAL

The casual or social friend is your light-hearted, fun-loving girl! She's the one who pops into your mind the moment you start planning a party, girls' night, or any gathering where good vibes are required. You know she'll show up sparkling — literally and figuratively — bringing energy, laughs, and probably the best shoes in the room.

She's the friend who shares your love of fashion, fun, and all things fabulous. And let's be honest, she looks like someone you could really let into that deeper part of your heart. On the surface, she checks all the right boxes and definitely brings a smile to your face. She might even have the potential to be something more — but here's where we stick to the golden rule of the friendship pyramid: vet before you invest.

She may be the one who never misses a mimosa brunch, but will she show up for the ditch-diving, messy-life moments? That's a whole different RSVP. And it doesn't mean she's not amazing — it just means she may not be *your* person for the deeper stuff. Let me tell you, a few glasses of bubbles can blur those lines! So keep it light and fun until time and experience reveal whether there's more under the surface. It does start to feel a little like dating, because friendships require the same amount of discernment. It may not be that deep, but it also may be worth finding out. If you are sensing a deeper connection, allow this casual friend to show you what she is made of and how your core values might line up outside of a social gathering. If you find yourself caring more, pay attention to your conversations and keep it light before sharing anything too personal. Too many times, I have been sucked in to feeling a bond with someone new and then spilling my life story before really knowing where the friendship was headed. Girl, let me tell you, the pain of that regret is worse than having a root canal! Oversharing with someone who has not earned your trust can cost you some unwelcome suffering. Be wise and enjoy casual conversation without the need to dive any further. Share your favorite music, fashion, food, movie, or book (*Bring It On* by Jen Morgan!). Enjoy this stage of friendship and what it brings to you at the moment. There's absolutely nothing wrong with having a circle of casual girlfriends. They expand your social world without the weight of expectations and add just the right amount of spice to your friendship recipe.

CHAPTER 2: THE FRIENDSHIP FOOD PYRAMID

THE BESTIE

Ah, the bestie. Need I say more?

At one point in my life, I didn't think I had to. A bestie was a bestie — through and through. She was the ride-or-die, the lifer, the one who held the deep secrets and gave the wink at the inside jokes only we knew. The BFF title felt sacred, simple, and solid.

But in recent years, the word has taken on new weight. I've even found myself shying away from it altogether. Why? Because somewhere along the way, the label started to feel a little too loaded. It began to create a hierarchy, the unspoken totem pole that put one woman above another. And if I'm being honest, that just doesn't sit right with me anymore.

I'm not in the business of ranking women, and I certainly don't want to unintentionally hurt those who mean so much to me but may not carry the title of *bestie*. Experience has taught me that the label *bestie* is sacred. It shouldn't be tossed around lightly. It carries a depth that goes far beyond the carefree friendships of my younger years — when I thought someone was a bestie, only to later realize she was a casual companion in disguise.

In our modern, social-media-saturated world, it's easy to throw around the term *bestie* like confetti. Simply snap a cute selfie, caption it "out with the bestie," and move on, without giving much thought to the weight those six little letters carry.

The bestie category in our friendship pyramid holds a depth that far outweighs that of an acquaintance or a social friend. This isn't just someone you grab coffee with or invite to your birthday brunch. The bestie has earned her place, and it's a sacred one.

She's stood the test of time, trial, and truth. She's shown up in both the highlight reel and the behind-the-scenes chaos. She holds your trust like something holy, and you hold hers the same. She's not just fun; she's a pillar. Her presence is marked by loyalty, honesty, grace, and a mutual alignment in values that ground your relationship in something real.

This isn't a simple title; it's a space reserved for someone who mirrors the very qualities you hold dear. And in most cases, she doesn't just reflect your values — she lives them too.

Mind you, we all have a different definition of what those qualities should be, and you'll have the opportunity to dive a little deeper into what those are at the end of this chapter.

A bestie holds a different place in our lives and possesses attributes that stand out among the rest. These qualities have been analyzed and challenged but have stood the test of time.

CHAPTER 2: THE FRIENDSHIP FOOD PYRAMID

What are some of the qualities a bestie should possess? It is different for all of us. What I crave in this type of relationship could be very different than what you crave. Through my research, I have learned that there are a few common traits that most women are seeking.

1. **Trust and loyalty.** Obvious, right? Trust and loyalty are the protein and carbs and every other macro of friendship! Besties are the ones we trust and can fully rely on. They are the keepers of our secrets and have proven they will show up when we need them the most. Ponytail and sweats, makeup or no makeup, tissue box or shirt sleeve, they are ready for it! They are the ones who answer the phone in the middle of the night and never make you feel like it was a burden. You know that secrets shared with her go to the grave, and she's not afraid to speak the truth — even when it's the last thing you want to hear. Having this trust and honesty reciprocated is essential.

2. **Emotional support.** Besties provide emotional support with empathy and patience. Being able to provide a secure feeling of comfort to each other is equivalent to our much-needed "healthy fats" in our health routine. The feeling you both get knowing you can lean into whatever circumstances you are facing is one of safety and warmth. You both have your own unique personality and form of expression, but when supporting each other emotionally, I encourage you to do your best to speak in her love language, not your own. This is an important quality to

look out for when determining what place a woman will end up holding in your heart.

A bestie has patience and has learned *you*. She has taken the time to learn unique qualities about you that others have not — both strengths and weaknesses. I cannot stress enough how important this quality is. As grown women, we are so multifaceted that we can be strong one moment and have a total meltdown the next over something that seems completely random. That does not make you less strong, smart, or anything else; it makes you human! Your bestie recognizes that about you, and you recognize it about her. It is a no-judgment zone where you spill all the tears like a blubbering fool and follow up the next day with an apology text, and she just gets it — no explanation needed.

These "bestie gems" are hard to find, so when you find one, make sure to nurture the friendship with care. Here is the great news: you may be blessed to find more than one! Your squad, your core four, your tribe — whatever you choose to call them, make sure you treat each one according to their individual, unique personality, and cherish them. Let's take Phoebe, Rachel, and Monica from *Friends* as a perfect example of this. Three dynamic women, each bringing their own distinctive personalities to a bestie friend group. They don't value one higher than the other, but they celebrate the beauty that separates them in the very best ways. If you find yourself blessed to have this, do a little dance, because it's pretty awesome!

CHAPTER 2: THE FRIENDSHIP FOOD PYRAMID

Are you ready for the big bestie caveat? A good friend can sometimes be confused with a bestie. Or a bestie can be confused with a ditch diver. As a matter of fact, *bestie* has somehow lost its meaning because it has been used so often and so lightly to describe a seasonal good friend that we're no longer sure what the limitations are and when to put our guard up. Girls, be intentional about honoring the meaning of friendships! Be intentional about categorizing properly so you can build healthy boundaries. Be intentional about the friendship pyramid, and take the time to assess and identify accurately. This can include friends shifting positions in the pyramid. It may be that someone held the bestie role in your life, but with time, she no longer possesses the same values and qualities you require to keep her in that category. Friend breakups are a thing, y'all, and they are not easy or fun. Just like romantic breakups, friend breakups involve a wide range of emotions, including sadness, confusion, anger, and grief. Especially when it involves betrayal of your trust or "ghosting." As you'll read in upcoming chapters, the loss of a friend can be almost as painful as the loss of a loved one through death. But don't allow the fear of suffering to imprison you in an unhealthy "bestie-ship." If the relationship has grown toxic, with some form of control, isolation, or manipulation, I encourage you to have those uncomfortable conversations in order to move on. I will never encourage simply cutting someone off, especially if she has held a treasured space in your life, but I am saying to pay attention to who occupies that position in your life. Trust your intuition when you're feeling distance or discord, and have the tough discussions that can lead to resolution, even if it means going separate ways. This is not an easy thing to do, but if she is in your bestie tier, you might be surprised how it can give new life to your relationship.

INTIMATE/FAMILY #DITCHDIVER

This one is a special breed! It is very difficult to speak about the ditch diver without tearing up. In my book *Bring It On*, I go into detail about what a ditch diver is. If you have not picked up the book, I strongly recommend you do. It will bring so much more clarity to the thread of this book and how I came to this place of letting go and allowing my emotions to heal.

Among all the friends you have, the ditch diver is the friend who has become family by choice. The ditch diver possesses more depth than most friends because she has walked with you through troubled waters. Most would say it's because she has walked with you the longest, but that is not necessarily true. There are ditch divers who have walked less time but possess more loyalty and depth and choose to meet you in the stage of life you're in. The ditch diver and the bestie can definitely fall into the same category, filling you up like mom's homemade lasagna, and that's when you've hit the jackpot!

CHAPTER 2: THE FRIENDSHIP FOOD PYRAMID

Luckily, for me, Jesus is my absolute best friend and ditch diver. He is the first place I turn in my times of surrender. He expressed it so well in the book of John:

> These things I have spoken to you, that in Me you may have peace. In the world you will have tribulation; but be of good cheer, I have overcome the world.
> **(John 16:33 NKJV)**

This is such a restful assurance He gives us in His Word! He is faithful to help us through every one of our troubles, and one of the ways He does that is by giving us the gift of friendship. He will place ditch divers in our lives to connect with at a deeper level, allowing us the space to be vulnerable, broken, or strong.

Although the ditch diver has already checked off all the boxes, this friend possesses even more depth and authority in our lives. She is the one who will speak truth in love, even when it hurts. She's that salty/sweet combo we crave. She is the one who will confront you with the freshly polished mirror when you have spiraled. She is the one who will get a hold of God when you don't have a prayer left in you. Yes, she will be with you at parties, social gatherings, and community functions, but she is also the one who will throw off her heels, roll up her sleeves, and jump in a ditch with you when you have nowhere else to turn. In other words, if the enemy is coming after you, he'd better think again, because you are not alone!

> As iron sharpens iron, So a man sharpens the countenance of his friend.
> **(Proverbs 27:17 NKJV)**

How is that Scripture verse relevant to us in this context? By sharing our strengths and wisdom, we are empowering our friends to be better. Our sword is sharpening her sword. We are removing masks and judgment, and we are lifting up the other person. Furthermore, we serve as a shield when the enemy tries to attack with thoughts of negativity, sadness, depression, anxiety, and so many other lies the devil attempts to sling at us when we are vulnerable. Every time you deposit a positive word by speaking something nice or sending a word of encouragement via text, you are protecting her. My day can be completely turned around when one of my ditch diver besties sends me a funny meme, an old time-hop photo, or a Scripture verse that speaks to the very thing I'm going through. My heart lights up, and immediately I experience the joy of knowing that this woman (or women) knows the depths of my soul, and I know hers. That is just the icing on the cake — hence the sweetness of dessert in our pyramid. God calls us to a higher commitment with these women, these ditch divers. He calls us to nurture and protect their hearts as well. In my case, these remarkable women come in the form of my four vastly different and unique sisters. Because of the span of years between us and our individual challenges in life, we are not always in tune with one another ; however, we are all 100 percent confident that when one of us

CHAPTER 2: THE FRIENDSHIP FOOD PYRAMID

is falling or broken, the other four will drop everything to be by her side. We are ditch divers by blood. My "Panther Posse" is another group of ladies who have filled my soul with so much joy through the years. They are ditch divers by choice, as we've been together since elementary school. Through our twenties and thirties, some of us even lost touch for many years, but once we reunited, it was like a day hadn't gone by, and the bonds were quickly formed once again. Though separated by many miles, we are deeply connected through our profound love and true concern for one another. We have been bonded by memories made since childhood, but more recently, we are tied together by something so much stronger — the love and loss of one of our own. The ditch divers show up, cry all the tears, rejoice in the 45 years of memories, and pray for peaceful days ahead.

Thankfully, God has continued to bless me with ditch divers as I mature into the woman and friend He has created. He has given me the knowledge of how to discern between varying types of friendships and how I can be my best self in every scenario. I fail regularly, but having these ditch divers to soften the blow of my imperfections will continue to be a blessing. One of the most basic ways I have learned to protect my heart and theirs is by simply being kind. This most basic behavior is the core of successful relationships. It's as if this level of friendship is an emotional bank account. Every act of kindness and every expression of gratitude and empathy is deposited into this account, and the more you deposit, the more you can withdraw when you need it the most. Sometimes, I find myself in serious debt.

Another way of protecting the other's heart is by being a good listener. Pay attention! For some, it's hard because we are so easily distracted and carry multiple topics of conversation at a time. Pay attention, show empathy when needed, and avoid giving unsolicited advice. A huge indicator of a ditch diver friendship is the confidence you share that your secrets are safely tucked in the vault. That should be on a "Friendship 101" list somewhere!

I don't know about you, but for me, trust is my main protein in friendship! If you can't keep a secret, you are unqualified to be my ditch diver. We are grown women, and we need to have the maturity to understand the importance of being a vault for our friends — and that includes pillow talk with the hubby. You can apply full transparency all you want about your personal life, but not about your friend's personal life. Few women have that kind of discipline and capacity, so I am calling you higher so you can be that friend. Shut. The. Vault. End of story!

Ah, ditch divers are a God send! I can't imagine doing life without amazing, strong, and loyal friends who bring their DNA to the mix. Female friendships are powerful! When you take the time to assess who you want to do life with and vet them into the right category, you will be surrounded by a force to reckon with!

CHAPTER 2: THE FRIENDSHIP FOOD PYRAMID

JOURNAL REFLECTION: THE HEART OF FRIENDSHIP

It's never too late to make new friends. It's never too late to deepen the ones you have. And it's certainly never too late to pause, reassess, and lovingly rearrange your friendship pyramid — placing people in the right category for your current season.

When we were kids, friendship was simple. We ran outside, jumped into a game of four square, or handed someone the other end of our jump rope. It was effortless. But now? Now we're tasked with something deeper: discerning who's showing up just for the photo op and who's willing to meet us in the muddy, messy ditches of life. We're in the business of protecting our hearts.

So take a moment. Breathe. Reflect.

What are the most important qualities you look for in a friend? What qualities do you bring into your friendships?

Here are my top qualities, shared to inspire you as you reflect on your own. Take time to pray about the traits you truly need in this season, and consider writing them down to create your own personal friendship pyramid.

- **Loyalty:** The unwavering assurance that your name is safe, even in your absence.
- **Grace and Forgiveness:** The ability to extend mercy and compassion when things get hard.
- **Empathy:** Someone who listens to understand, not just to respond.
- **Truth:** A friend who speaks with love, even when it's hard to hear.
- **Presence:** Not just physically there, but emotionally *with* you.

LET'S TAKE IT A LITTLE FURTHER

- **A Heart for God:** She is someone you can share kingdom-minded values with.
- **Consistency:** She shows up, reaches out, and stays connected.
- **Honesty:** She tells the truth, even when it's uncomfortable.
- **Supportiveness:** She celebrates your wins, holds space for your losses, and never sees your shine as a threat.

CHAPTER 2: THE FRIENDSHIP FOOD PYRAMID

CONCLUSION

Friendship isn't about popularity. It's about proximity to the heart. And you, my friend, deserve the kind of relationships that nourish your soul, not just your social calendar.

Be intentional. Stay true to your friendship pyramid. Manage all your friendship macros with care, because love, loyalty, and trust are nutrients your heart can't live without.

Reflections

If you were to create a friendship app, what features would you include?

Chapter 3

Grief In Life and Death

Grief was not on my agenda that morning. I had just stepped out of the shower, towel wrapped tight, steam fogging the mirror like a veil. I wiped it clean, and as I did, I felt I was also wiping away the version of myself I no longer wanted to be. I was ready. Ready to be the kind of friend I've always needed. The kind I'd prayed for. But just as I was walking in that fresh sense of purpose, loss came knocking at my heart, loud and uninvited. Not the death of a loved one, but the quieter kind. The loss of friendship. Of history. Of laughter that now just echoes. It was a different kind of grief, but it was still grief. We usually tie grief to death, but grief doesn't always wait for a funeral. Sometimes it creeps in when someone chooses distance. Or when conversations go silent. Or when someone you thought would always be there just isn't. The dictionary might call it sorrow caused by loss. But it's also the ache of disconnection, the sting of change, and the weight of what could've been. And if you've ever sat in that kind of silence — you know. You've felt it too.

Many of us have grappled with the darkness and turmoil that comes from a deep loss. Unfortunately, this type of despair seems to have been a thread throughout my life. I don't say this coming from a pity-party mindset; I'm just authentically stating the facts. When suddenly faced with the reality of the newfound absence of friends, I immediately spiraled to a place of emptiness and grief. I did not know that kind of grief existed. I would have never associated grief and friendship. I would never have paired them together, but I've become all too familiar with the fact that the two go together like wine and cheese. Really bad wine and moldy cheese. If you've read my book *Bring It On*, then you know how grief, specifically sudden tragedy, is something I am very familiar with and how it is an integral part of my story. Mourning losses has molded who I am and taught me how to cope in different situations. I didn't choose to become an expert in the topic; it chose me. However, grief in the form of broken friendships was an unexpected plot twist. It blindsided me and led me down a path of rediscovery — one I didn't necessarily ask for. God has a funny way of doing that.

CHAPTER 3: GRIEF IN LIFE AND DEATH

For many years, I feel the Holy Spirit has guided me in the way of openly sharing parts of my life to help others grow or even just to connect in ways they otherwise would not. It has always brought me so much joy to write, lead, and share. Mostly, because I feel my transparency is a way for other women to be vulnerable while serving as a tremendous form of therapy for me. When I initially got serious about writing my first book and taking my mission of inspiring women to social media and living out loud, I felt empowered. However, I was quickly advised by other women in ministry that once I put it out there, I also needed to be prepared for people leaving. I innocently thought this could never happen to me — maybe to others, but surely not me. My girls have my back and will continue to support me, no matter what. Much to my surprise, I was wrong! The reasons are irrelevant, but I did find out how wrong I was, and it was crushing. I may never know the real reasons why some chose to move on, but I have and will always stand firm in the fact that I am flawed. I fail. I disappoint and am imperfect in so many ways. But one thing I am also confident in — if you're in my life, I will actively listen and do my best to grow from those imperfections if given the opportunity. (That goes back to the mirror we talked about earlier!)

I understand life happens and how consuming the demands of life can be; it can drain us of the energy required to maintain relationships. But to be ghosted by another person is simply another level of heartbreak — one I don't wish on others. I had to know if I was alone in this rare, lonely space. I had to know if there was anyone else experiencing the same realization. So in my research, I conducted a survey by reaching out to several women of various ages. I had to know, so I asked!

- Do they have the same circle of friends as they did growing up?
- Are they surrounded by strong women, willing to be ditch divers?
- Do they have a group of ladies they can be transparent with?
- What is their definition of friendship?
- What does it take to be in it for the long haul with female friendships?
- Is the pain of letting someone go worth missing out on the value and joy they once brought to your life?

I was astonished to discover I was not alone in experiencing the "friendless nest." I was not the only one whose life was in a different place. Take a moment to answer these questions for yourself. Self-reflection can be very enlightening.

Experiencing grief is not limited to losing a loved one in death, although it is the ultimate form of grief. Feelings of grief can also be associated with losing a job, social status, financial stability, divorce, moving out of state, and various other factors, including the aging process. You may even find yourself grieving the woman you once were! To paraphrase the beloved Carrie Bradshaw, sometimes you have to release who you once were to make room for who you are meant to be.

CHAPTER 3: GRIEF IN LIFE AND DEATH

GRIEF IS PERSONAL

The depth of pain associated with our personal sorrow is not open to being measured by others. Period. It is a very personal experience based on the individual's own emotions. Only the person experiencing it knows the depth of their anguish and how they feel about their loss. Grief cannot be categorized based on the relationship with the other person either; it is based solely on how the person experiencing the loss feels. For instance, animal lovers grieve the loss of their pet with the same intensity as they would a human loss. However, others who don't share the same love for animals may trivialize the loss and not understand their pain. It is not for anyone to judge or determine how you should feel about these types of losses. Grief is personal.

In my life, I have tragically lost three older brothers, beginning when I was just eight years old and the most recent being in May of 2020. These traumatic losses have each been embedded in my heart forever. Each death created different memories and growth experiences for me as a person. Nothing can prepare you for the absence of someone you deeply love and care for. Each occurrence was very personal for everyone affected. There are healthy and unhealthy ways to deal with loss, and let me tell you, I experienced my fair share of both. Specifically, when my brother Paul passed away in 2008. At the time, I was working and doing my best to raise three very active kids, as Kevin was working hard and traveling on business three to four days a week. Life was hectic, not to mention our marriage was already on rocky ground. When I got the call about Paul, I was immediately triggered back to my childhood, when my oldest brother, Mark, died in a car accident. The PTSD was real, y'all, but I didn't recognize it at the time. I dove into a place of darkness, and I did what a lot of people default to, which was to numb the grief with alcohol and prescription drugs. I was spiraling, and so was my marriage. I did not have the proper tools in place to appropriately recover from this devastation. I didn't know how to find peace because God was not at my center. I was not going to Jesus to help save and mend me, and I certainly wasn't allowing the Holy Spirit to guide me in the grieving process. My journey was painful to me and everyone around me, but thankfully, the Lord is a redeemer, and I am here to tell you this story with a clear mind and grateful heart.

The more my life unfolded, the more I felt myself relating to Ruth in the Old Testament. Consider this quote from the *One Step Closer Bible*, a version narrated by Candace Cameron Bure, in which she so eloquently describes the book of Ruth this way:

> What do you do when life caves in? What do you do when everyone seems to be against you? Then, as you're still reeling, life suddenly deals you another harsh blow, another tragedy. Now what do you do? Do you run away, crawl inside yourself, lock out the world? Is there anything left to live for? The book of Ruth is the story of what one young widow did

CHAPTER 3: GRIEF IN LIFE AND DEATH

when life dealt her one tragedy after another. It is a story of challenge and inspiration for each of us who faces circumstances beyond our control.

EXCHANGE GRIEF FOR GRATITUDE

The phone call I received in 2017 was yet another time when I felt myself being cut off at the knees. One of my dearest friends of over ten years was suddenly in the hospital with very little hope of making it. *God, can this be real? Am I losing this woman whom I have grown so close to? Am I losing this woman who has become like a sister to me? How can I possibly manage this grief?* I'll be honest with you; it took me a long time to navigate the loss of Robyn. It emotionally paralyzed me for months, even a couple of years. It was a long time before I could fully allow her absence to penetrate my soul. The main difference in healing through this pain is where I was in my life and the personal growth I had achieved through those years. Having prayer consistently as a part of my daily life made all the difference; I spent quiet time daily talking to God and to people who allowed me the time and space to mend my wounds. Filling voids with positive people, music, and writing were the tools I needed to heal in a way that eventually led me to a place of gratitude for having Robyn in my life when I did. Instead of allowing myself to spiral into self-sabotage, I eventually learned to embrace my memories with my dear friend. I filled up with photos and songs and the beautiful memories at the forefront of my mind daily. Besides my incredibly supportive and loving husband and my family, another key piece to my journey was the close women I had by my side. These are the women who stuck together as we endured the loss of our sister in friendship. Each of us was coping in our own very personal way, but we still knew that we were in it together. We were never going to judge one another, and we were confident in the fact that if one of us fell, the others would be there to pick us back up. Outside of my relationship with God, knowing that they were there was my security blanket in a time when I felt naked and vulnerable.

> Don't ask me to leave you and turn back. Wherever you go, I will go; wherever you live, I will live. Your people will be my people, and your God will be my God. Wherever you die, I will die, and there I will be buried. May the Lord punish me severely if I allow anything but death to separate us.
> **(Ruth 1:16–17 NLT)**

Unfortunately, those women are no longer in my life, and the heartache it brings me cannot be accurately depicted in words. I can only say it has left an overwhelming hole in my heart. I am much better than I was a few years ago, after the epic 50th birthday party, but if I'm honest, I am still a work in progress at finding peace without the women with whom I anticipated growing old. In my mind, we were like family. Now my goal is to remain grateful for the years I had with them. All the laughter, the fun, the tears, the trips, the time with our families — all of it! I am grateful, and I am blessed that I was surrounded by wonderful people who found ways to fill me up in times I felt empty. I pray I did the same for them. I will forever be grateful for their friendship throughout those years.

BEING SELECTIVE WITH YOUR TEARS

When you're walking through grief, one of the most important things you can do is protect your heart. And I mean really protect it. Not with walls, but with wisdom. Everyone handles grief differently, and not everyone in your life will know how to walk with you through it. Some people, even those who love you, may not have the emotional maturity or experience to hold space for your pain. They may try to help but end up saying things that sting more than soothe.

You've probably heard all of the classics before:
Time heals all wounds
Everything happens for a reason.
You just need to move on.

It's okay to acknowledge that not everyone is equipped for this part of your journey. That doesn't make them bad people; it just means they're not the ones you need to lean on right now. Give yourself permission to protect your grief. You can still love people from a distance while choosing to share this sacred, vulnerable space with those who can truly support you.

That brings me to this: Don't go through it alone. Whether it's a trusted friend who has experienced deep loss, a family member who listens without judgment, or a professional grief counselor, talk to someone. Let your heart be seen. Grief can be incredibly isolating, and having someone who understands — who won't rush you or try to fix it — can make a world of difference. And yes, you might find yourself repeating the same story or the same questions more than once. That's normal. That's healing. The right people will understand that your process doesn't need to be neat or linear. These are the people in your pyramid we talked about earlier.

Grief is painful. It's messy. It's sacred. But it is also something that heals. It doesn't stay this sharp forever. Be patient with yourself in the process. Speak kindly to your heart. And remember that you are not alone in this.

Grief and gratitude — two emotions that seem like opposites, even contradictions. And yet, during a quiet conversation with my dear friend and writing partner, Diana Acosta, she shared her personal journey through grief in a way that brought the two together with grace and honesty. Diana has a beautiful gift for weaving Scripture into our work — not as an expert or theologian, but as someone who lives what she writes. Her words struck a deep chord with me,

CHAPTER 3: GRIEF IN LIFE AND DEATH

and I knew they belonged in these pages. I asked her to share that part of her story here so that you, too, might find strength, comfort, and clarity through her faith-filled lens.

DIANA'S STORY

In March 2022, everything shifted with one life-altering text: "Brannon died in a motorcycle accident." No prelude. No phone call. Just a cold text. I felt like I had been hit by a bulldozer — gasping for air, weeping uncontrollably, paralyzed by disbelief. On St. Patrick's Day, Brannon was killed by a drunk driver. The pain was immense. The grief, consuming. He was deeply loved. At his memorial, seventy-five motorcycles revved their engine in unison to honor him, and inside the chapel, we wept. Brannon wasn't just my friend — he was an absolute rock star, and someone who loved Jesus boldly.

Barely two weeks later, I received a message from a longtime friend with more devastating news — my mentor, Pastor Wiley Jones, had passed. He wasn't just a mentor; he loved me like a daughter. Another sharp blow to a heart already bleeding.

Then came April. Still grieving both losses, my daughter called from California. Gently, she said, "Mom... it's Benny. Benny Lopez." I collapsed in sobs. Benny was like a spiritual son. I had watched him grow from a young man into a powerful man of God, a devoted husband

and father. On April 12, 2022, the Lord called him home. My heart couldn't take any more.

And then came May. Another phone call. Another friend. Another loss.

I felt numb. I couldn't cry anymore. The pain was too deep.

That's when God met me in my despair and said something that changed everything: "You cannot keep carrying pain on top of pain. I want you to exchange your grief for gratitude." At first, it didn't make sense. Gratitude? For loss? But in His presence, surrounded by peace only He can bring, I understood. He wasn't asking me to be thankful for their deaths — He was asking me to be grateful for their lives. For the memories and the impact they had on my life.

So I started writing. I wrote what I loved about Brannon — how he challenged me and brought joy to every room. I did the same for Pastor Wiley — his wisdom, elegance, and fatherly love. I remembered Benny's laugh, his bold faith, and his humor. The tears still came — but now they were mixed with warmth. With purpose.

Gratitude became my healing balm. It didn't erase the pain, but it transformed it. *Every time a wave of grief hit, I fought back with gratitude. I spoke it out loud. I chose to feel it. And little by little, sorrow gave way to peace.*

CHAPTER 3: GRIEF IN LIFE AND DEATH

Friend, I won't say it was easy. But I decided to obey what God placed on my heart: to let gratitude lead the way out of grief. It doesn't mean you forget; you remember with love, joy, and gratitude.

If you're grieving, I encourage you to try this: exchange your grief for gratitude. Not for the loss, but for the gift of having had them in your life. It may not happen overnight. But if you keep turning your heart toward gratefulness, healing will come. I promise — it will.

I love Diana's powerful story! I, too, have had to exchange grief for gratitude in the absence of friends I once loved and cared for so much. It was difficult for me to apply this principle since most of my absent friends are living and breathing. I had to surpass the hurt and grief that came along with their withdrawal, and to wish them well. I finally understand there is nothing wrong with me; life simply changes, and so do others. I speak words of gratitude and blessings over them, as I redirect my emotions of "friendlessness" — if that is even a word. If it is not, then allow me to create it to describe my 50's.

In any relationship, it's important to distinguish between loving a person for who they are and loving the way they make you feel. The same holds true for grief. It may be time to ask yourself, "Am I grieving them or the way they made me feel?" Either way, I assure you, grief will soon pass and be replaced with fond memories.

Reflections

Reflect on a time when you have had to grieve a lost or broken friendship.

_____
_____
_____
_____
_____
_____
_____
_____
_____
_____
_____
_____
_____
_____
_____
_____
_____
_____
_____
_____

Chapter 4

Oils of Renewal

By Diana Acosta

As we explored in the previous chapter, friendship and grief often intertwine in unexpected ways. It's not something we prepare for or hope for, yet when we love deeply, we inevitably open ourselves to the risk of deep loss. That's the cost of connection and the proof of how meaningful it truly was.

FIFTY & FRIENDLESS

My dear friend and writing partner, Diana Acosta, understands this intersection of friendship and grief on a profound level. It's one of the many reasons our bond runs so deep. We met in 2020 while working on my first book, *Bring It On,* and instantly clicked. Although our stories are different, we quickly discovered we share something sacred — we've both been entrusted with grief. Not just the grief that follows death, but the quieter grief that comes through broken friendships and unexpected goodbyes.

Diana brings so much to this chapter — not just as a writer, but as a woman of strength, wisdom, and unwavering faith. With a background as a life coach, speaker, and former pastor, she has spent years pointing people toward hope in Jesus. Her love for the Lord is powerful and contagious, and her life is a testimony to the beauty of walking through pain with purpose.

She inspires me with her relentless pursuit of healing, self-awareness, and joy. Diana doesn't run from her reflection — she meets it with boldness, honesty, and grace. It is with deep admiration and love that I introduce her to you here, as she shares a transformational part of her story.

CHAPTER 4: OILS OF RENEWAL

THE EYES ARE THE WINDOW OF THE SOUL

In 2007, I avoided the mirror. Any time I had to look at myself in the mirror, it was followed by deep sighs and contempt. My hair was polished, my make up was flawless, but I did not like the woman staring back in the mirror. I was not used to seeing a woman who within seconds would cry just by looking at her own eyes. They say the eyes are the window of the soul, and at the time, there were no truer words. I would look into my eyes, and although my lashes were on point, pain stared back at me. A deep pain that screamed at me for help.

My soul was shattered, and my heart was hanging on for dear life after being broken by divorce. Mind you, it was my decision, so some would say it was self-inflicted pain, but I strongly disagree. I would argue that having the courage to walk away from a toxic situation is not for the faint of heart, although it hurt more than anything I have ever experienced.

This was my introduction to what I now understand as grief. Not grief in the way we typically think of it, but grief in its rawest form: the ache of watching something sacred fall apart.

Grief was not a foreign word to me in theory. I had read it, heard it, even spoken about it before. But this? This was the first time I felt it in my bones. Deep, heart-wrenching sorrow unlike anything I had ever known. The day my family was broken, grief became my daily companion.

The pain caused to my children is something I will continue to work through until I can stand before the Lord. Not because He has not healed our hearts, but because there are things within a family that are irreplaceable. It cost them the version of family they knew. It altered the safety of their world. To this day, I wish I could have spared them the pain.

Few things make me cringe more than when people say that children are resilient. They are not. They may weather the storm, but they will suffer the pain and insecurity that comes along with it. Will they grow up to be productive adults? Absolutely! But they don't deserve the journey and process of getting there, along with the voids they will encounter later in life. I can boldly say this in hindsight not because I wish to be back in my marriage but because I wish we could have provided a better foundation for them. They deserve it. They will always deserve it.

THE MIRROR SCREAMED

Looking in the mirror became a quiet torment. It wasn't just my reflection that troubled me; it was also the silent scream in my eyes that I could no longer silence. The discomfort ran so deep, I convinced myself that maybe a change in appearance would help. So I dyed my hair. I updated my wardrobe. I curated a new version of myself, hoping that maybe — just maybe — if the outside looked different, the inside would follow! Nope. That did not work.

CHAPTER 4: OILS OF RENEWAL

No shade of lipstick or new hairstyle could touch the ache I carried. The pain wasn't skin-deep; it was soul-deep. And my eyes, the windows to a weary, grieving heart, kept revealing the truth I was trying to hide. The truth was that I was grieving. I was grieving what I lost, who I had been, and the life that had unraveled before me.

And yet, somehow, that mirror became sacred ground. Because the woman who stared back at me, broken as she was, was also brave. She was standing at the threshold of a painful, holy transformation. What felt like an ending was, in fact, the beginning of something beautiful.

I DID NOT SIGN UP FOR THIS

The transformational work of Jesus in our lives can't be confined to a timeline or squeezed onto a vision board. What we dream up for our future often looks nothing like what God has in mind, especially if we haven't yet mastered the art of absolute surrender. (Spoiler alert: I haven't!) Every time I've told the Lord, with full conviction, "Take the wheel!" I somehow manage to grab it right back and steer in my own direction. "How's that worked for you, Diana?" Not great. I always end up back at square one. And so will you, until you give Him full control.

God's plans are always good — and always in our best interest — even when they involve pruning. Yep. That word. *Pruning* sends a chill down my spine every time, because I know all too well the kind of pain it brings. In some circles, they call it a trigger, and for me, it brings up the ache of many losses. But when God is the one doing the pruning, even though it stings in the moment, it's always with purpose. It's always for our good.

I'm no different than most women. I still believe in the fairy-tale ending, and I'm hanging on until the wheels fall off or Jesus calls me home. Whichever comes first! But I've learned the hard way: life isn't a fairy tale. Even at its best, the road can be bumpy, sometimes even brutal, before we ever reach what we think is our happily ever after. And let's be honest: even that definition is different for everyone. For some, it's status or success. For others, it's a strong marriage, lifelong friendships, or a sense of deep inner peace.

In this journey of losses and gains, I've discovered that the loss of friendship hits just as hard as any other kind of grief. Like Jen, I've experienced my share. Some friends have gone to be with the Lord. Others have faded due to distance or differences. Either way, it hurt. Deeply.

In one single year, I faced a list of losses, including friends I considered sisters. And when I say that, I mean it. I don't use that term lightly. I could spend pages trying to explain the causes of those losses, but doing so would only drag me back into the emotional trenches of rejection, betrayal, and disappointment.

CHAPTER 4: OILS OF RENEWAL

Instead, I chose differently. I let myself grieve. I gave space to the sorrow. And then I made a bold, intentional decision: to become the kind of friend I crave!

I looked back at each of those relationships and asked myself what they brought into my life, both the beauty and the lessons. And now, with every step forward, I strive to show up better, wiser, and more prepared for the friendships still ahead.

What does that mean exactly? It means you've got to take an honest look in the mirror and ask yourself the tough stuff.

- Are you being intentional about the relationships in your life?
- Are you vetting the people you allow into your personal space or just letting folks pull up a chair without an invitation?
- How well are you stewarding the gift of friendship?
- And let's not forget the most important one: What are *you* bringing to the table?

Becoming the friend you crave doesn't start with other people — it starts with you. It starts with taking inventory of your own life, your habits, and your heart, and being brave enough to ask the hard questions. And when I say *ask*, I don't mean thinking about it for thirty seconds while scrolling your phone. I mean sitting down with paper and pen in hand. Go ahead; light a candle if it helps. Get honest. And if you're not quite sure where to start, don't worry — we've got you. Just flip to the end of this chapter. No excuses.

Bring your questions to God — the ones you're afraid to ask the people who may not be equipped to speak into this season of your life. After all, who knows you better than you and the One who created you?

God will always shine light on the areas that need work — not to shame you, but to shape you. He is never in the business of condemnation. His truth comes wrapped in kindness and covered in grace. It may not always feel good in the moment, but it will always lead you toward freedom. His peace will guide you as you make those small, necessary shifts toward the version of yourself that reflects His love.

That's the version of you that becomes the friend you crave. The spouse you hope for. The coworker, the leader, the sister, the mentor — whatever role you're called to step into. It starts with brutal honesty and the courage to let God refine you from the inside out.

Why does this matter so much? Because after gut-wrenching loss, you can't afford to live on autopilot. You are now responsible for stewarding your own heart, your relationships, and your decisions with intentionality. Wisdom must become your closest companion

CHAPTER 4: OILS OF RENEWAL

if you want to become the kind of friend and person you truly desire to be.

There are areas of your life you simply can't leave unattended. And I'm not talking about how you look. Outward appearance is the easy part. What takes real strength is doing the internal work — the heart work.

> The heart is deceitful above all things, And desperately wicked; Who can know it? I, the Lord, search the heart, I test the mind, Even to give every man according to his ways, According to the fruit of his doings.
> **Jeremiah 17:9–10 (NKJV)**

The "heart" in this passage represents your mind — your thoughts, emotions, intentions, and choices. It's the root of your behavior and the filter through which you process life. No one introduces themselves by saying, "Hi, I'm battling jealousy, anger, and a whole lot of bitterness." Yet many go through life never acknowledging what's really going on beneath the surface. And unfortunately, those hidden issues eventually leak out, often sabotaging relationships that were meant to be a blessing.

Becoming the friend you crave requires hard work. It demands that you do the deep work of transformation by allowing the Holy Spirit to shine light on the toxic patterns and blind spots that are keeping you stuck. Think of it as a soul cleanse. A spiritual gut detox. Call it whatever floats your boat, but don't ignore it!

When I think about doing the deep work, choosing inward refinement over surface-level change, I can't help but reflect on the story of Esther. Her transformation was both internal and external, and it was done with purpose, preparation, and obedience. If you're not familiar with her story, I urge you to read it in full. It's a masterpiece on preparation and purpose, inside and out. Powerful story with a major plot twist!

THE FAIRY TALE

At first glance, Esther's story reads like every woman's fairy tale. A beautiful young woman is chosen in what appears to be a royal pageant to become the next queen for King Ahasuerus. Out of all the young women in the land, she is selected to wear the crown and ultimately becomes the vessel God uses to save an entire nation.

Sounds glamorous, right? It's often taught that way, especially in Sunday school or surface-level devotionals. But when we look beyond the crown and into the heart of the story, we find a reality that looks far less like a fairy tale and far more like a woman who knew grief deeply.

CHAPTER 4: OILS OF RENEWAL

EVEN QUEENS GRIEVE

Before she was queen, she was a daughter who had lost everything. Esther became an orphan at a young age, living through the grief that comes from losing both parents. Though her older cousin Mordecai lovingly raised her as his own, we cannot ignore that there is no substitute for the nurturing embrace of a mother or the guidance of a father, especially in a young girl's formative years.

Then came the decree.

Young virgins from across the provinces were gathered and brought to the king's palace in Shushan. And let's not overlook the fact that Esther was taken. She didn't volunteer. She didn't sign up for it. She was removed from the only family she had left, from the only familiar place she knew, and placed in an environment filled with uncertainty and unfamiliarity.

Can you feel the weight of that moment?

She went from grieving the loss of her parents to grieving the forced separation from Mordecai. And now she's being prepared for a man she did not choose. What looked like a glamorous opportunity on the outside was a painful stripping away of everything she had known.

While Esther was externally groomed to appear before the king, something deeper was happening internally. She was being refined, tested, and prepared, not just to win a crown but also to fulfill a divine calling. It was not a simple makeover; it was a full year of preparation.

>Esther 2:12 (NIV) says:

>Before a young woman's turn came to go into King Xerxes, she had to complete twelve months of beauty treatments prescribed for the women, six months with oil of myrrh and six with perfumes and cosmetics.

>The NKJV calls it "preparations for beautifying women."

This wasn't simply about physical beauty. This was about process. Separation. Transformation. Twelve months of waiting, wondering, and becoming. Not only did Esther endure it, but she also allowed herself to be positioned by it. That's the power of preparation. That's the cost of purpose.

CHAPTER 4: OILS OF RENEWAL

AROMATHERAPY WITH PURPOSE

Essential oil of myrrh holds deep spiritual significance, especially within Christianity and Judaism. Often referred to as an anointing oil, it has historically been used for sacred purposes, including praying for the sick (James 5:14–15).

The oil of myrrh is derived from the sap of tree trunks and goes through a steam distillation process, producing a smoky, bittersweet aroma. It's complex, much like the process it represents. Esther spent six months being treated with oil of myrrh, a preparation intended to soften her skin before she was presented to the king.

HOW DOES THIS APPLY TO US?

If we're truly committed to becoming the best version of ourselves, becoming the friend we crave, we must be willing to go through our own "oil of myrrh" process. Figuratively speaking, it means allowing God to soften the rough edges in our lives, refine our character, and purify our motives.

We cannot continue treating people however we want and expect to maintain healthy relationships. We can't call it "transparency" or "just keeping it real" when what we're doing is speaking carelessly and wounding others. Stewarding our words and our actions is part of spiritual maturity. And that stewardship applies not just when people are present but also in their absence.

It's hard to love someone genuinely when you've been speaking negatively about them. It's hard to give a warm smile and an enthusiastic hug when bitterness has been brewing behind the scenes. It's hard to enjoy someone's presence when you've torn them down in their absence.

If we want authentic, lasting relationships — friendships that are life-giving — we must let the Holy Spirit apply the "oil of myrrh" to our hearts. It softens. It heals. It prepares us to show up with love, integrity, and grace.

Years ago, I had to confront a friend I loved deeply. Her behavior was unpredictable — some days she was warm and lighthearted, and other days, sharp and standoffish. One day, I kindly asked if she had any close female friendships growing up. She admitted she hadn't. Raised with brothers, she spent most of her time around guys and had never really bonded with women.

And suddenly, it all made sense.

She had never taken the time to baste in the "oil of myrrh" — doing the inner work required to soften the rough edges. She hadn't yet embraced the process of self-reflection and refinement that makes true friendship possible.

CHAPTER 4: OILS OF RENEWAL

So let me ask you:

- What are you doing to soften your demeanor?
- What intentional steps are you taking to be the steady, safe, and kind presence on the other end of the phone?

Now, I'm not suggesting you fake it or be "drippy sweet" — because if it's not authentic, it won't last. But you can be kind. You can be thoughtful. You can be the friend who listens, who shows up, who speaks with grace even when it's hard. And yes, you can be loyal — especially when loyalty costs something.

Some of these qualities don't come naturally for everyone. They take work. Sometimes, they require you to sit with some uncomfortable truths about yourself — to recognize the patterns that push people away and to decide, boldly, *This is not who I want to be anymore.*

It takes surrender — real surrender. The kind that says, "God, I can't change myself without You." And then you let Him go to work. You let the Holy Spirit smooth out your tone, heal your insecurities, and shape your character into something truly beautiful.

And yes — it might require a mirror.

JEN MORGAN

SIX MONTHS OF PERFUME AND PREPARATION — THE SPA LIFE

Some translations of Esther's preparation describe it as involving "shavings" — something we all understand to be essential in smoothing and beautifying.

I'll never forget the first time I waxed my legs. I was a waxing virgin! A friend swore waxing was better than shaving — it removes the hair from the root, she said, so the smoothness lasts longer. What she conveniently failed to mention was the part where it feels like your soul is being ripped from your body!

There I was, laid out on the waxing table, when the aesthetician gently told me to close my eyes and "relax." Ha! I felt something warm on my legs, and suddenly she ripped off the paper, and I screamed! I think they may have heard my scream on another continent. Yes, my legs were smooth. Yes, the smoothness lasted much longer, but oh, did it hurt!

That moment taught me something bigger than how to endure beauty rituals. It taught me that if I want to live at a higher level of excellence, I must let God go for the root, not just the surface. Sure, we can occasionally fake a smile. We can fake kindness. We can show up polished for likes and approval. But when God begins a real work in us, He doesn't stop at what people can see. He goes straight for the root of bitterness, jealousy, insecurity, pride, and shame, those quiet toxins that sabotage us from within.

And yes, it stings. But oh, it's worth it.

So how do we let God do the deep cleansing? We start with His Word. If you take nothing else from this chapter, take this:

> For the word of God is living and active, sharper than any two-edged sword, piercing to the division of soul and of spirit, of joints and of marrow, and discerning the thoughts and intentions of the heart. **(Hebrews 4:12 ESV)**

His Word doesn't just inform — it transforms. Where there's sadness, He brings joy. Where insecurity lingers, He whispers affirmation. Where anger and envy have settled, He uproots and heals. This isn't about being religious or chasing aesthetic spirituality. This is about heart work. You can spend your time scrolling through social media and picking up cute memes and one-liners referring to God, but it does not come close to spending time in His Word. His Word will shed light on the toxicity within. He will call out what is not working for you even if it hurts, and trust me, it will hurt. He will expose unhealthy friendships and relationships, calling you higher. Trust me when I say if you don't let go willingly, He will yank them out of your life, and it will hurt. It will hurt for a while. Then it will hurt no more, and it will be the best thing that ever happened! Once you get past the sting, you will see things for what they really are and be so thankful. God does not mess around! He loves you too much to leave you raspy and "as is." He wants the best for you, and He will stop at nothing to make you the best version of yourself so you can turn around and be the friend you crave!

Esther's preparation lasted a full year. Twelve months of process before walking into her divine assignment — and eventually saving a nation. Who's to say your process isn't preparing you for something greater too?

After years of my own journey of healing, refining, and surrendering, I can finally look in the mirror and love the woman staring back at me. I've grown to love her quirks, scars, and sassy sense of humor. I don't just admire her lashes; I finally see joy in her eyes! Life has returned to her soul. And for that, I'm grateful. Grateful for the bittersweet journey of the "oil of myrrh." For the refining fire. For the wax strips and all!

Because today, I can say it with confidence: I am the friend I crave.

Reflections

What are some of the "rough edges" you'd like to smooth out in order to be the friend you crave?

_____
_____
_____
_____
_____
_____
_____
_____
_____
_____
_____
_____
_____
_____
_____
_____
_____
_____
_____
_____

Chapter 5

Fashion, Forgiveness, and Letting Go

What I truly appreciate about Diana is not only her deep insight, but also her sense of humor! She weaves humor into her communication, and then she skillfully drives home her point. Recently, she shared a funny story about a pair of shoes that perfectly encapsulates the tone of this chapter. One of her friends surprised her with a stunning, high-end pair of strappy sandals.

Being the shoe lover she is, she eagerly accepted the gift, despite the shoes being half a size too small. To remedy the situation, her friend insisted she use a stretcher overnight! I can't help but smile as I share this — because it's something I could see myself doing. So there she was, placing the shoes in a stretcher overnight, hoping for a miracle fit.

In the morning, to her relief, the sandals fit perfectly! She was thrilled to flaunt her new strappy sandals, but just an hour after leaving the house, the thrill was gone — her feet began to swell from the tightness, with her toes poking out of the edges of the shoes. She went back and told her friend what happened, and her friend's solution was to give the stretcher another try. It's no surprise why these two are such good friends — both are shoe lovers!

After leaving the shoes in the stretcher for a few days and hoping for a better fit, she eagerly tried them on again. This time, they felt much more comfortable. However, after a couple of hours, her feet swelled again. This time, she was getting even more irritated! She was determined to make it work. Taking the stretcher, she tightened it to the max, only to hear snapping straps — the shoes broke under pressure! Now getting them fixed would likely cost a pretty penny, all for the sake of ending up with a shoe that's still half a size too small.

The lesson learned through her story is profound: sometimes, despite the allure of expensive, name-brand items, they simply

CHAPTER 5: FASHION, FORGIVENESS, AND LETTING GO

aren't the right fit. In this case, there was absolutely nothing wrong with the shoes — they were just a half-size too small for her. They may have been a perfect fit for someone else with slightly smaller feet. However, she persisted in trying to make them work, even though they weren't meant for her.

This lesson resonates beyond the realm of footwear and can be applied to various aspects of our lives. It speaks to the importance of recognizing when something isn't the right fit and being willing to let go, even if it seems valuable or desirable. In the context of friendships, as we've been exploring, it speaks to the significance of knowing when a friendship is no longer for us. Just as not every pair of shoes fits every foot, not every person who enters our lives is meant to be a friend.

As we delve into the dynamics of friendship and the love and acceptance that healthy relationships offer, it's essential to refer to our friendship pyramid from the previous chapter. This framework reminds us that it's our responsibility to define what we seek in a friend and to carefully discern what aligns with our current season of life. Not everyone who crosses our path is destined to become a friend or stay well beyond their welcome. When we fail to carefully vet those we welcome into our lives, we risk "snapping" what was never meant for us and causing pain to ourselves and others. Recognizing this reality is the first step toward understanding the importance of releasing what no longer serves us. Letting go is a challenge, particularly for individuals like me, who tend to persevere until the wheels fall off! However, it can be liberating and lead to personal growth, paving the way for healthier, more like-minded relationships and experiences in the future.

Friendships are meant to enrich our lives, providing companionship, support, and joy. However, not all friendships are healthy or beneficial. Sometimes, we find ourselves in toxic friendships that drain our energy, cause us emotional distress, and hinder our personal growth. In such cases, letting go of the friendship becomes necessary for our well-being and happiness. In this chapter, we'll explore the challenging but essential process of recognizing toxic friendships and gracefully letting them go. We'll draw from the story of my friend who stretched beyond the limits, resulting in the ruin of a beautiful pair of shoes.

LET'S TALK THE "F-WORD"

Within the realm of friendship, the "F-word" is frequently misinterpreted and extended beyond its intended significance. Now, relax, I'm not about to curse! I'm referring to *forgiveness*. Forgiveness is the "F-word" we often misapply and stretch in order to maintain what worked twenty years ago or to remain loyal to someone who helped us a decade ago but has since proven to be disloyal. We frequently use forgiveness as a means of sidestepping necessary conversations that might be uncomfortable yet could

CHAPTER 5: FASHION, FORGIVENESS, AND LETTING GO

potentially lead either to a breakthrough or to the end of a relationship.

Forgiveness is inherently virtuous. As Christian women, we are called to forgive and extend forgiveness to others when we've been wronged. However, there's a risk of misusing forgiveness as a crutch to avoid standing up for ourselves or fostering healthy friendships. Too often, we rationalize away blatant behavior by saying these kinds of things to ourselves:

- "She didn't mean to say that."
- "Maybe she wasn't in a good mood; she's going through a lot."
- "Perhaps she had one too many and didn't realize what she was saying."

Do any of these excuses resonate with you? They certainly do with me, as I've used forgiveness as a blanket to cover the obvious. While forgiveness is crucial in any relationship, it becomes problematic when it's exploited or taken for granted. Yes, we should forgive others for their transgressions, but when someone persists in hurtful behavior and disregards the value of the friendship, it becomes our responsibility to establish necessary boundaries to safeguard our hearts.

LETTING GO WITHOUT SNAPPING THE STRAP

Just the mere thought of this topic makes my heart sink! This is a challenging area for me because I'm the type of person who believes there's a solution for every problem, just so I can avoid letting go. I'm that girl who sets out to declutter my closet every year, only to end up keeping almost all the same clothes because I simply can't bear to part with those beautiful dresses or those jeans that used to fit perfectly but now barely zip up! I'll rationalize keeping them by convincing myself that they'll fit again when I lose those extra pounds, or that they were so expensive, it would be wasteful to discard them — surely, they'll fit again someday.

Instead, I should adopt a realistic approach, acknowledging that I wore them well and with pride. And, ladies — sadly, this does include handbags that take up a huge amount of space! I'm sure many of you can also relate to holding onto that one pair of jeans you just can't seem to let go of. They fit perfectly maybe five years ago, but now they're just taking up space in your closet, preventing room for new, better-fitting clothes.

Many of us are long overdue for a spring cleaning in our personal lives too. There are people who may have perfectly fit our lives years ago but no longer fit today. Either we've drifted apart due to life's demands or we have evolved into different individuals over the years, no longer sharing the same passions or beliefs. In fact, we shouldn't be the same person we were twenty or thirty years ago.

CHAPTER 5: FASHION, FORGIVENESS, AND LETTING GO

We should constantly be growing and evolving — and the people we choose in our lives should also be growing.

So how do we determine when it's time to let someone go from our lives? How can we recognize when we're clinging to a memory of what our friendship used to be, thus depriving ourselves of the possibility of a vibrant, joyful friendship in the present?

One of the key signs it's time to let go is unchanged behavior. This is a clear sign! In other contexts, it would be considered a red flag. If that person is staying stuck in their past habits and behaviors that are affecting the friendship, it's time to let them go. Let's explore some other telltale signs:

1. **Constant negativity:** A friend who consistently criticizes, belittles, or attempts to dim your spark can significantly impact your self-esteem and confidence. They may not express it directly but do so through subtle, incremental actions or remarks. Sometimes, they may disguise their criticism by claiming they were just joking and that you're too sensitive. A true friend should always be mindful of your feelings and prioritize protecting your self-esteem rather than undermining it. However, this doesn't mean they should constantly shower you with empty compliments or withhold the truth. There's a significant difference between constructive feedback and underhanded remarks. As the saying goes, when someone constantly talks to you about others at the table, you will likely be discussed at another table. Let that marinate.

2. **One-sidedness:** In a healthy friendship, there's a balance of give and take. However, if you find yourself always giving without receiving much in return, it may be a sign of a one-sided or parasitic relationship.

3. **Manipulation and control:** Toxic friends may try to manipulate or control you, dictating your choices, isolating you from other relationships, or using guilt and coercion to get their way. Whenever someone repeatedly reminds you of something they did for you years ago, it can be a form of control.

4. **Lack of respect:** Respect forms the foundation of any healthy relationship. If your friend consistently disregards your boundaries, values, or feelings, despite you expressing your concerns, it's a clear indication of toxicity. It's important to remember that we cannot fault anyone for something we haven't communicated beforehand. If you've already shared your feelings and the disrespect persists, why subject yourself to it?

5. **Draining energy:** Spending time with a toxic friend can leave you feeling exhausted, emotionally depleted, and weighed down instead of uplifted and supported. This is a significant issue for me personally. Have you ever experienced leaving a gathering feeling heavy, as if you can't shake off the negativity? That's not okay with me. While spending time with friends is usually one of my favorite activities, leaving feeling drained is not worth it. I would prefer to be alone. I understand that in the span of a friendship, not every

CHAPTER 5: FASHION, FORGIVENESS, AND LETTING GO

moment will be perfect, but if you consistently find yourself feeling this way, it's crucial to reassess where and how you invest your time and energy.

If any of these aspects resonate with your situation, alongside your own observations and assessments, and there's no change in behavior, it's a clear sign that it's time to let go. This is where forgiveness and grace play crucial roles. When you reach the point where you recognize that there's nothing more to be done, the initial step is to forgive yourself first. It might surprise you that I'm beginning with what appears to be the hardest to do, but forgiving yourself is key.

Forgive yourself for the role you played in allowing things to progress further than necessary. Forgive yourself for your part in the friendship not evolving as you had hoped. Remember, it takes two people to nurture a relationship. If the friendship soured or simply didn't meet your expectations, take the time to reflect on your contribution and grant yourself forgiveness. Challenge yourself with tough questions about your involvement and extend grace to yourself initially. Showing yourself grace before even considering anything else will make all the difference in the outcome.

I understand this might seem counterintuitive, but it's crucial. You cannot extend forgiveness and grace to others if you're unable to offer it to yourself. This isn't a selfish act or an excuse for unhealthy behavior; it's a fundamental principle that will foster healthy closure.

When you're questioning how to move forward, shower yourself with grace and fill your own cup with forgiveness, allowing yourself the ability to extend forgiveness to the person you're prepared to let go of. If that entails taking a day away from it all to reflect and pray about your emotions, then do so. You are worth it! Remember, the friendship also holds value, regardless of how it may have turned out now. You might find it helpful to involve another trusted friend in the process of this reflection. They could assist you in articulating your thoughts and provide prayerful support as you navigate through any grief it may bring. The key idea here is that experiencing forgiveness yourself is crucial before extending it to others. If you struggle to forgive yourself, you may not be fully prepared to offer forgiveness to someone else.

In the Gospel of Matthew, you'll encounter a well-known Scripture verse. It's often quoted with the emphasis on loving one's neighbor while ignoring the importance of loving oneself. Let's read it carefully:

> And the second is like it: 'Love your neighbor as yourself.'
> **(Matthew 22:39 NIV)**

This verse is part of Jesus' response to a question about the greatest commandment, underscoring the significance of both loving God and loving others. It emphasizes the principle of treating others with the same care, respect, and kindness that we desire

CHAPTER 5: FASHION, FORGIVENESS, AND LETTING GO

for ourselves. In essence, we cannot give what we don't have. If we struggle to love ourselves enough to offer ourselves forgiveness, how can we expect to love others enough to extend forgiveness to them? It all begins with how we treat and value ourselves.

We all have unique ways of coping with loss and the process of letting go. Personally, I've found it challenging to let go due to the numerous losses I've experienced in my life. However, through these experiences, I've learned to prioritize self-love and have discovered helpful techniques to protect my heart. Here are a few practices that have been particularly beneficial in enabling me to forgive myself and to ready my heart for letting go:

1. **Acknowledge your feelings:** Allow yourself to acknowledge and validate your feelings about the friendship. It's normal to experience a range of emotions, including sadness, anger, guilt, and relief. However, when you approach how you feel from a place of forgiveness and grace, the experience changes. You can let go without feeling resentful or holding a grudge.

2. **Have a direct conversation:** When you feel comfortable and fully prepared, initiate an honest and respectful conversation with your friend about your decision to end the friendship. Express your feelings calmly, focusing on "I" statements rather than blaming or accusing them. By the time you decide to have that conversation, it's likely they

are also prepared for it. Ending a friendship doesn't happen overnight, and if it has been deteriorating for some time, chances are the other person won't be blindsided by it.

3. **Create distance:** Sometimes, it's necessary to create physical or emotional distance from a toxic friend to protect your well-being. This may involve reducing the frequency of interactions, unfollowing them on social media, or limiting communication altogether. By this, I don't mean ghosting them altogether. If they were your friend at one time, they are familiar with your patterns of behavior as well, and ghosting someone is not an act of the best version of you. Create some distance, and if creating distance still does not get the message across, then it is best to have a conversation. I am a huge believer in talking through differences and making a mutual decision to cut ties or work to heal together.

4. **Seek support:** Surround yourself with other supportive friends, family members, or a therapist who can offer encouragement, validation, and perspective during this challenging time. Lean on your support network for emotional guidance and reassurance.

An excellent book that may aid in the process of letting go is *Necessary Endings* by Dr. Henry Cloud. This is an excellent resource

CHAPTER 5: FASHION, FORGIVENESS, AND LETTING GO

to aid us in understanding ourselves first and then preparing to let go.

Letting go of a toxic friendship is a courageous act of self-preservation and self-respect. While it may be painful and difficult at first, it opens the door to healthier, more fulfilling relationships and a greater sense of inner peace and authenticity. It will open up a bigger space in your heart, similar to adding another shelf in your closet for those new arrivals.

By recognizing the signs of toxicity, setting boundaries, and prioritizing your well-being, you empower yourself to move forward with confidence and grace, knowing that you deserve friendships that uplift and inspire you.

As the relentless, hopeful friendship romantic that I am, I want to emphasize once more the importance of thoroughly considering all factors before making a final decision. You may not share my approach, and that's perfectly okay, but personally, I won't consider ending a friendship without giving it my all first. I'm hoping you will do the same.

I vividly remember trying on a designer dress in my closet every few months, stubbornly hoping that this time it would finally zip just right! I would wiggle on the bed, attempting to zip it up, and then stare in the mirror, wishing that the material would stretch and be forgiving, but it never did. Then, one day, during a closet clean out, I felt it was time. I was ready to happily give it away to someone else who would wear it well! I was able to let it go.

Are you aware that by holding onto a friendship that no longer suits us, we might also be hindering the other person's growth and potential to find another friend?

Ask yourself: "What if the pain of letting go is simply the doorway to the joy of finding your place among women who truly understand you?"

I encourage you to remain steadfast in who you are when someone has chosen to walk away from you. When they choose to adjust the terms of the friendship without an honest and upfront conversation, it should tell you everything you need to know. Do not stop being unapologetically you with your head held high. This will allow the right women to enter your life at just the right time.

In 2 Samuel 12, we read of King David's reaction after his child became ill. I have always found this Scripture passage to be profoundly impactful. It speaks about hope and eventual acceptance, despite the initial anguish and fervent prayers for healing:

> And the Lord struck the child that Uriah's wife bore to David, and it became ill. David therefore pleaded with God for the child, and David fasted

CHAPTER 5: FASHION, FORGIVENESS, AND LETTING GO

and went in and lay all night on the ground. So the elders of his house arose and went to him, to raise him up from the ground. But he would not, nor did he eat food with them. Then on the seventh day it came to pass that the child died. And the servants of David were afraid to tell him that the child was dead. For they said, "Indeed, while the child was alive, we spoke to him, and he would not heed our voice. How can we tell him that the child is dead? He may do some harm!"

When David saw that his servants were whispering, David perceived that the child was dead. Therefore David said to his servants, "Is the child dead?"

And they said, "He is dead."

So David arose from the ground, washed and anointed himself, and changed his clothes; and he went into the house of the Lord and worshiped. Then he went to his own house; and when he requested, they set food before him, and he ate. Then his servants said to him, "What is this that you have done? You fasted and wept for the child while he was alive, but when the child died, you arose and ate food."

And he said, "While the child was alive, I fasted and wept; for I said, 'Who can tell whether the Lord will be gracious to me, that the child may live?' But now he is dead; why should I fast? Can I bring him back again? I shall go to him, but he shall not return to me."
(2 Samuel 12:15–23 NKJV)

I understand that the loss of a friendship pales in comparison to the loss of a child, but I use this as an example of hope and resolution. Once you've exhausted all efforts to nurture a friendship and you've tried everything you know to salvage it, but the relationship remains stagnant, then it's time to pick yourself up! Ahead lies a lifetime of potential great friendships for you. Lingering in one that is not fruitful, joyful, or beneficial deprives both you and others of the opportunity for genuine connection.

There is no greater joy than spending time with a friend whom you love and who loves you back! Surround yourself with Scripture passages that remind you of the importance of being a good friend and cultivating healthy friendships. Pray for good friends to enter your life, and pray for the qualities they should possess that resonate with you. Pray for their hearts, that they may love you in the way you need to be loved. Yes, it's okay; you can pray for healthy relationships to manifest in your life!

CHAPTER 5: FASHION, FORGIVENESS, AND LETTING GO

Here are a few Scripture verses to write in your journal, post on sticky notes, and place wherever you need reminders that God cares about friendships:

> A friend loves at all times, and a brother is born for a time of adversity.
> **(Proverbs 17:17 NIV)**
>
> One who has unreliable friends soon comes to ruin, but there is a friend who sticks closer than a brother.
> **(Proverbs 18:24 NIV)**
>
> Two are better than one, because they have a good return for their labor: If either of them falls down, one can help the other up. But pity anyone who falls and has no one to help them up.
> **(Ecclesiastes 4:9–10 NIV)**
>
> Greater love has no one than this: to lay down one's life for one's friends.
> **(John 15:13 NIV)**
>
> As iron sharpens iron, so one person sharpens another.
> **(Proverbs 27:17 NIV)**

Most importantly, glean wisdom from your friendship experiences. Undoubtedly, there were valuable lessons learned throughout that friendship journey. I am confident you learned a lot about yourself during that process. Consider creating a new approach or revisiting the friendship pyramid outlined in our previous chapter. This can assist you in organizing your thoughts and identifying your needs for future friendships.

The journey of letting go of a friendship and finding new ones can be both challenging and liberating. It takes courage to acknowledge when a friendship is no longer serving us and to make the decision to move forward. Yet in doing so, we open ourselves up to the possibility of forming deeper, more fulfilling connections with others.

Embracing forgiveness and grace, both toward ourselves and others, is key to healing and moving forward. Ultimately, the journey of letting go and finding new friendships is a process of self-discovery and growth. And through this journey, we can find solace, joy, and fulfillment in the bonds we form along the way.

"I don't know what I would have done so many times in my life if I hadn't had my girlfriends. They have literally gotten me up out of bed, taken my clothes off, put me in the shower, dressed me, said, 'Hey, you can do this,' put my high heels on and pushed me out the door!"
~ Reese Witherspoon

CHAPTER 5: FASHION, FORGIVENESS, AND LETTING GO

"I still have friends from primary school. And my two best girlfriends are from secondary school. I don't have to explain anything to them. I don't have to apologize for anything. They know. There's no judgment in any way."
~ Emma Watson

"A day without a friend is like a pot without a single drop of honey left inside."
~ Winnie the Pooh (A. A. Milne)

"A friend is one soul abiding in two bodies."
~ Aristotle

Reflections

What does it look like to release a friendship you thought might last forever? Do you feel lighter in letting go?

_____
_____
_____
_____
_____
_____
_____
_____
_____
_____
_____
_____
_____
_____
_____
_____
_____
_____
_____
_____

Chapter 6

Table for One, Please!

Imagine walking into an upscale restaurant, with your heels clicking confidently on the floor, and approaching the host with a confident smile. Dressed in your favorite outfit, whether it be a pair of jeans and your new trendy heels or a long, flowing dress, your presence exudes self-assurance as you warmly say, "I'd like a table for one, please." Your tone is calm, your gaze is fixed, and your stride is unlike anything you have experienced before. As your demeanor radiates a humble strength, the women in the room are captivated by admiration and intrigued by your confidence. They quickly turn inward, wondering if they can do the same, inspired by your example.

What they don't know is that at one point in time, you would have wondered the same thing. You would have been equally impressed by another woman's confidence, thinking it could never be you — until you discovered *you*. Until you finally learned to love the woman in the mirror and made her your best friend!

This kind of confidence doesn't happen overnight. It grows in the soil of self-acceptance. It blooms when you finally embrace the woman you've become — the one who has grieved friendship losses, learned to discern what relationships are life-giving and which ones are draining, and figured out how to be the kind of friend you used to long for.

Isn't that what we've been doing together on these pages? That thread you've felt running through this entire book — it's been leading you back to *you*. The best friend you didn't know you had.

As we approach the conclusion, **the most significant takeaway I can offer is the importance of being your own best friend.** It might sound like a cliché, but without embracing this incredible individual — YOU — and all that she has experienced, you cannot authentically embody her. By embracing the woman who walks with you every day and choosing to love her, accept her, and evolve alongside her, you are becoming the most confident woman you have ever been.

This may feel daunting at the beginning, since some may misinterpret your confidence, especially in a society saturated with narcissism and over inflated egos. But once you fully become your own best friend, you are not moved by what others think or say; you are focused solely on being a healthy, vibrant version of yourself. Once you practice rooting for yourself, you'll be pleasantly surprised to discover that the right people will root for you as well.

I hear you, girls! You want me to answer the big question: "How do I become her? How do I become this vibrant, amazing woman?"

It starts with embracing your journey of self-acceptance and self-appreciation. You are worthy of your own admiration and support. Being okay with yourself and walking in confidence means embracing your true self, flaws and all, and understanding that you are enough just as you are. It's about silencing the inner critic and celebrating your unique journey, with all its highs and lows. When you accept yourself fully, you radiate an authentic confidence that isn't dependent on external validation or comparisons to others. You stand tall, knowing that your worth is inherent and not defined by societal standards. This inner assurance allows you to navigate the world with a sense of peace and purpose, unshaken by the challenges you encounter. Walking in confidence means trusting your abilities, making decisions that align with your values, and facing each day with a resilient spirit, knowing you are perfectly imperfect and beautifully human.

You also need to peel off the connotation that loneliness and depression are the driving forces behind "table for one" or "party of one." That is simply not true! Quite the opposite, in fact — it is a season of celebration! It's when you can slip into that outfit that's been hanging in your closet, tags still attached, waiting for its moment, and you grab those scissors, saying, "Today is the day!" There's no specific occasion, no invitation, no party bus — just you and all the mountains you've conquered. Now that's freedom! That is confidence! The "party of one" season is the time to do things that fill your soul with joy and to intentionally do these things for yourself and by yourself.

Consider these ideas that may fill your soul with joy:

- Volunteering for a nonprofit organization
- Taking a long walk or discovering new ways to move your body
- Playing with new recipes
- Prayer
- Being still in the quiet
- Going to the movies
- Trying new restaurants ("Table for one, please!")
- Going to a party with no plus-one

CHAPTER 6: TABLE FOR ONE, PLEASE!

- Movie marathon on the sofa
- Taking the trip on your bucket list — solo

To be honest, this has never been easy for me. I still battle a severe case of FOMO when I find myself alone on a Saturday night. Kevin and I used to have our calendar filled to the brim, and if it wasn't full, we'd take the initiative; often, people would join us.

But now, in my 50's, as my social life has dwindled, I've found myself questioning what went wrong. Negative self-talk tied me in knots, wondering where I took a misstep. However, I've come to believe that God was trying to tell me something different. He has more in store for me. My efforts to bring people together were sometimes ways of avoiding being with Him. Unfortunately, those parties, fun outings, and large group events sometimes ended up being distractions. After all, the enemy distracts when he cannot destroy.

The phrases "table for one" or "fifty & friendless" have become a play on words for me. I can't express enough gratitude for the incredible women who surround me. They're a support system of intelligent, fun, inspiring individuals whom I thank God for every day. He strategically placed each of them in my life for a specific purpose, just as He did with me in theirs. They know who they are, and I can confidently say they fulfill every parameter of my pyramid. God doesn't make mistakes. These small circles that have formed around me are magical and meaningful, and I cherish each of these relationships deeply.

"Table for one" symbolizes my comfort in my own skin. It's about being okay with being with myself, in the quiet moments and the calm. I'm less preoccupied with why someone has exited my life, assuming it's something I did wrong, and more focused on pleasing Jesus. I want to continue answering His call to inspire women to unmask, unveil, and unleash their purpose. My insecurities are gradually fading, and because of that, I can hold my head high and truly be the friend I crave — not just to myself but also to the women I'm fortunate enough to cross paths with along the way.

I am fully aware that the term "table for one" sounds like a solitary term or one exclusively for a single person. But in the context of being your own best friend, "table for one" is a state of being. I am a married woman who often chooses the company of my husband and my three kids to spend most of my quality time with. But I also choose the company of myself in those quiet moments, and I have learned to be my own best friend. Well, for the most part, anyway! I may still be polishing some of those rough edges, but I have come a long way. And so can you. Transforming from a self-proclaimed extrovert and morphing into being an introverted extrovert is huge, and it has taken a while to grasp. But it is possible, and I'm living it now because I'm learning to love my authentic self. Not because I have it all together, but because I've learned to love myself through my own journey, including my mistakes. I believe that when we can love ourselves through our experiences, we become more relatable to others and empathetic to where they may find themselves.

CHAPTER 6: TABLE FOR ONE, PLEASE!

I fondly remember an experience I had with a woman who looked at me from afar and believed I had it all together. She opened her heart to me at a women's study I was leading. In her eyes, my life was a seamless blend of success, social vibrancy, and personal fulfillment. She often saw me at events, engaging with others, always "put together," and exuding an air of unshakeable confidence. She looked at my lifestyle and thought I had the perfect life. To her, it looked like I navigated life's challenges with ease, always surrounded by friends and never missing a beat. She admired my apparent balance and poise, thinking I had mastered the art of living. Little did she know the internal struggles I faced, the nights of self-doubt, and the effort it took to maintain that facade. In our time together during Bible studies I was leading, I openly shared my hardships, the grief I endured, and the ghosts of the past I silently wrestled with. It was important for her to see that life is not picture-perfect, and it will not always be filled with joy.

Once I shared my story, her demeanor changed. She felt accepted. She felt I was relatable. I didn't know my life looked intimidating to her from afar, and I didn't realize the impact my transparency would have on her. I am so thankful that God gave me the words and the strength to openly share my journey with her.

Have you ever felt intimidated by someone else's self-confidence? You don't have to answer that by raising your hand! You can answer by showing vulnerability and grace and deciding to love yourself through it.

Flee the temptation of comparison. Flee the temptation of self-deprecation. Embrace the amazing woman you are, with all the wealth of experiences that only you possess. No one else on this God-given planet has experienced all the unique things you have. No one else has walked the same path you have walked, down to your first steps and losing your first tooth! You may think it sounds funny or exaggerated, but if you really think about it, you own your memories! Take ownership of your experiences!

- What stops you in your tracks?
- What makes you feel empathy?
- What makes you relatable to someone else?

You lived it, and now it forms a part of how you respond, not only to things and to others, but primarily to yourself.

LOVE AFFAIR

How does having a love affair with yourself sound? I can hear the laughter in the air. What in the world is a love affair with self?

Having a love affair with yourself goes back to the journey of deep self-discovery and unwavering self-acceptance. It begins with recognizing your own worth and treating yourself with the same kindness and respect you would offer to a loved one. I am confident you would not speak to a loved one the way you sometimes speak

CHAPTER 6: TABLE FOR ONE, PLEASE!

about yourself. Hopefully, from reading the first five chapters of this book, you are invested enough to understand the importance of loving the woman in the mirror.

Embrace your strengths and acknowledge your flaws without judgment, understanding that they make you uniquely you. Take time to treat yourself to things that bring you joy and nurture your passions, and celebrate your achievements, no matter how small. Cultivate a compassionate inner dialogue, replacing negative self-talk with affirmations of love and appreciation. As you prioritize your well-being and happiness, you'll find that loving yourself becomes a natural, fulfilling experience, allowing you to navigate life with greater confidence and resilience. This love affair with yourself is the foundation for all other relationships, radiating positivity and attracting genuine connections into your life.

What does having a love affair with yourself look like? It is treating yourself the way you would like to be treated by others. It is not waiting on the couch for someone else to love you, take you out, show you a fun time, or say beautiful things. You intentionally choose to love yourself the way you need to be loved. However, it is not as easy as it sounds. Some women may think it's easy for me to say that because I am married and have a husband to come home to, while others may be single and don't have a companion waiting for them to say and do the things they want. Well, that is the whole point! Let me explain.

Having a love affair with yourself is enjoying your own company, whether you are married or not. Being single is a status, not a condition. Whether you are married or single, you must always remember that you were created in love, and loving yourself is a gift! There is nothing more attractive in a woman than confidence and self-assurance, not only romantically, but in all relationships, including the workplace. You can always tell how a woman feels about herself by the way she speaks, walks, and carries herself.

FLYING NOT-SO-SOLO

In October 2022, I embarked on one of the most exhilarating and nerve-wracking adventures of my life. I traveled solo to Italy to join a retreat with thirteen women I had never met. This journey began with a small nudge from an Instagram influencer I followed. At first, I dismissed the idea, thinking, "Travel to Europe by myself? That's crazy!" Yet every so often, I found myself clicking the link to admire the villa and explore the itinerary, only to close it quickly. One day, I saw there was a cancellation on the trip, and a room had opened. On a whim, I mentioned it to Kevin, and to my surprise, he was all in. "If it's something you want to do, go for it," he said, giving me his full support. Before I knew it, my deposit was paid and my flight to Rome was booked. I could hardly believe I was taking this giant leap of faith — by myself! Although I could have invited my daughter or a sister, I knew this journey needed to be alone. After navigating a year of challenging changes in friendships,

CHAPTER 6: TABLE FOR ONE, PLEASE!

I felt a divine push to step out of my comfort zone and rediscover myself. The Holy Spirit guided me to embrace this journey solo.

Upon landing at the airport in Rome, I met four of the women who were also part of the retreat. As we waited for the next leg of our trip, we chatted, and I immediately felt at ease. Their warmth began to melt away my fears.

As the group gradually came together over the first twenty-four hours, I became more comfortable with embracing my individuality without a sidekick or best friend by my side. I had no choice but to be myself and let God manage the rest. I was one of four women who had ventured on this trip alone, and it was incredible. Each day brought new adventures and memories in parts of Italy I had never seen before. It was magical. Every woman had a unique story and reason to allow herself to go on this retreat. At night, we enjoyed delicious dinners prepared by our personal chef at the villa, drinking wine in our pajamas, dancing, playing games, and opening our hearts to one another. Guards came down and masks came off. The food, scenery, history, and shopping exceeded all my expectations, but it was the heartfelt discussions and shared stories that truly made this the trip of a lifetime.

Returning home, I felt transformed. I felt like a woman who could spend days with people who had known me for years or with complete strangers. As long as I was comfortable and safe in my own skin, it didn't matter. Ladies, I promise you, the Jen who existed ten years ago could never have imagined embarking on a solo journey like this. Naturally, some women bonded more than others for several reasons, and I formed lifelong connections with a few of them. This deep bond made every moment of apprehension worth it.

I understand that not everyone can just book a trip to Italy or has the same courage to fly across the country in the name of self-discovery! My intention is not to set an unreachable goal but simply to share what I did to step outside my comfort zone. However, there are plenty of things you can do that don't require a passport. Being accountable to yourself as a woman involves taking proactive steps to ensure personal growth, well-being, and fulfillment. Here are some ways to achieve this:

1. SET CLEAR GOALS

Personal Goals — Define what you want to achieve in various aspects of your life, such as career, health, hobbies, and personal development. Don't be shy, and don't underestimate yourself! This is an opportunity to think big and take a shot.

Professional Goals — Identify your career aspirations and the steps needed to reach them.

- Do you have a professional mentor at work?

- Is there someone you can sit with for coffee and glean from their professional career?

2. DEVELOP A ROUTINE

Daily Schedule — Create a daily routine that includes time for work, prayer, self-care, exercise, and relaxation. Once you have created a routine, do everything in your power to stick to your routine by building discipline and structure in your life.

3. SELF-REFLECTION

Journaling — I love my prayer corner! Create a quiet space just for you to write about your thoughts, feelings, and experiences regularly. This helps in understanding yourself better and tracking your progress. I cannot stress this enough! This must be one of my favorite and most effective ways to keep track of my progress in life. I am always blown away by how God has worked on my behalf.

4. PRIORITIZE HEALTH

Physical Health — Find what you love and do it often! Mine is walking and Pilates. Maintain a healthy lifestyle through balanced nutrition, regular exercise, and sufficient sleep. This may sound redundant, but when you make it part of your everyday lifestyle and start reaping the benefits, you will make it a priority.

Mental Health — Take care of your mental well-being by managing stress, seeking therapy if needed, and engaging in activities that bring joy and relaxation. Be mindful. Never allow shame or embarrassment to deprive you of reaching out to a friend or loved one if you feel you are struggling. A lack of social support and isolation can lead to feelings of loneliness and depression. Instead, take the time to seek the support you need.

5. COMBATTING MENTAL HEALTH STIGMA

You don't need a degree to advocate for mental health; you just need empathy, openness, and discernment. Taking care of your mind is just as important as caring for your body or spirit. And while this may not be my professional lane, it is my personal conviction that your mental well-being matters. It's okay to ask for help. It's okay to not be okay. And it's more than okay to protect your peace while you're healing.

CHAPTER 6: TABLE FOR ONE, PLEASE!

Lastly, being accountable to yourself is being able to set up accountability partners. This may sound like a paradox. Being accountable to oneself includes others? Yes. It does. It is a way of protecting your own boundaries. Of course, you will need to be selective of whom you choose to be your accountability partners. Trust and confidentiality are key factors. Select someone you trust completely. You'll be sharing personal challenges and achievements, so confidentiality is crucial. Choose a partner who will listen without judgment and provide constructive feedback.

I would be remiss if I didn't mention that becoming your own best friend and flying solo for a season may mean that your accountability partner can be a professional. The essence of this chapter is embracing oneself! The core of this book is the realization that you may not always have a best friend by your side or a large social circle. Finding a trusted individual may not be in the cards for now. (It will not always be that way.) Do not discard the idea of having a counselor as a professional accountability partner or of joining a support group. They don't have to be your best friend, shopping buddy, or travel partner, but they can be someone who supports you and speaks the truth to you when needed. These groups can be found in churches, online, during in-person meet-ups, and elsewhere. Keep in mind the importance of vetting before committing.

JEN MORGAN

SPACE FOR YOU AND THE ULTIMATE FRIEND

Have you ever seen the movie *War Room*? If not, I highly recommend setting aside time for it. Brew a warm cup of tea or pour a glass of red, snuggle up in your favorite cozy blanket, and don't forget a box of tissues.

Released in 2015 and produced by Affirm Films under the direction of Alex Kendrick, *War Room* is more than just a film — it's a reminder of the power of prayer, intentional solitude, and spiritual strategy.

One of the most profound takeaways for me was the idea of creating a dedicated space for prayer — a personal sanctuary for reflection, surrender, and connection with God. While I may not have an entire "war room" in my home, I do have a sacred space: my prayer corner.

In that corner, I meet with God.

I cry there. I worship there.

I leave my burdens there.

And just as importantly, I pray for others there.

CHAPTER 6: TABLE FOR ONE, PLEASE!

On the wall beside me, names and prayer requests hang — some neatly written, others scribbled quickly in moments of urgency or heartbreak. As that wall fills up with petitions and intentions, it never feels overwhelming. It feels sacred. Because I know that every whispered prayer is heard by the One who sees all.

That space has taught me to embrace solitude without fear. When the world grows quiet and the crowd disappears, my prayer corner reminds me I'm never truly alone. God is always present, always listening, and always loving me with a depth I will never fully comprehend. His love meets me there. It rejuvenates me there. It strengthens me to go back into the world — even if I'm requesting a "table for one."

Because even then, I know I'm not dining alone.

I'm walking with the One who calls me chosen.

I'm sitting beside the One who knows my name.

I am never abandoned — I am always loved.

As you turn this final page, my prayer is that you create your own sacred space — physically or spiritually — a place where you remind yourself who you are and whose you are. May you embrace the quiet not as a sign of emptiness but as an invitation to deeper intimacy with God. May you walk boldly, whether in a crowded room or seated solo, knowing you are supported, seen, and deeply, unshakably loved.

This isn't just the end of a book — it's the beginning of a new chapter in your confidence, your wholeness, and your walk with God.

You've met your best friend on these pages.

Now go live like you believe it.

Table for one? Absolutely.

But never alone.

Reflections

Does a "table for one" frighten you or give you a sense of peace? What does a love affair with YOU look like?

_____
_____
_____
_____
_____
_____
_____
_____
_____
_____
_____
_____
_____
_____
_____
_____
_____

About the Author

Jen Morgan is a speaker, writer, certified grief coach, and encourager with a heart for women navigating the ever-changing seasons of life. Through her love of faith, family, and fun, she shares her own journey of loss, resilience, and rediscovery to inspire others to embrace the beauty of imperfection. Her first book, *Bring It On*, explored how faith carried her through life's greatest traumas. In *Fifty & Friendless: Table for One, Please*! Jen invites women to reflect on the power of friendship — especially the one we build with ourselves. She is a proud native of Cincinnati, Ohio, but her roots have been firmly planted in Texas for over twenty years, where she and her husband have raised their three children. She treasures her roles as mom, sister, and "ditch diver" for her friends.

www.ingramcontent.com/pod-product-compliance
Lightning Source LLC
Chambersburg PA
CBHW051131160426
43195CB00014B/2426